"That our Bible doesn't contain words like 'social media,' 'virtual reality,' or 'smartphone,' doesn't mean it has nothing to say about them and their use. By tracing our technological impulses and abilities to our creation as God's image bearers and exploring how the subsequent stages of redemptive history affect us and our technologies, John Dyer steers between poles to which we easily gravitate: uncritically demonizing or devouring technology. His sound biblical and theological reflection and thoroughgoing understanding of the history and philosophy of technology and media make him a reliable guide to readers who want to follow Jesus faithfully in the digital age. For years, I have used *From the Garden to the City* in the local church and university classroom. I'm thrilled that it has been revised and look forward to many more years of learning and teaching from it."

—**Keith W. Plummer**, PhD, dean of the School of Divinity and professor of theology at Cairn University

"I love this book with its overarching biblical metanarrative exploring the use of technology from the dawn of creation to new heaven and new earth. I love the careful differentiation between older tools and modern devices, and the changing effect on our bodies and our minds. The theoretical side is well handled with constant examples from Christian practice and discipleship. . . . This book will push you forward in your understanding of both technology and theology—and more importantly, into a deeper understanding of who you are as you seek to walk humbly with your God."

—**Pete Phillips**, director of the Centre for Digital Theology at Spurgeon's College

"This is the best book out there on the theology of technology. It shows how the Bible has a lot more to say about technology than you would think, and offers great advice on how to manage this spiritual force."

—**Kevin Kelly**, senior maverick, *Wired*

"*From the Garden to the City* is an essential read to equip Christians with a nuanced Scriptural and theological foundation for ethical living in a digital culture. With grace, curiosity, and precision, Dyer provides an accessible model for critical and faithful engagement with technologies that are radically changing us and the world."

—**Kate Ott**, author of *Christian Ethics for a Digital Society*, and professor of Christian social ethics at Drew Theological School

"In a day where we simply can no longer avoid engaging the pressing questions of technology, this new edition of *From the Garden to the City* is a welcome addition to ongoing theological and ethical conversations about how these tools radically alter and reshape every aspect of our society. John Dyer is a skilled, balanced, and hopeful guide who combines his many years of experience on both the technical and philosophical aspects of these important debates. Not only will you better understand the nature of technology, but you will also see how it is shaping how you view God, yourself, and the world around you—both for good and ill."

—**Jason Thacker**, author of *The Age of AI: Artificial Intelligence and the Future of Humanity and Following Jesus in a Digital Age*, and chair of research in technology ethics at The Ethics and Religious Liberty Commission

"Game-changing. Reading *From the Garden to the City* was the most important work in my early stages of theological and cultural analysis of technology, paving the way to me launching FaithTech. I literally keep a box of these books in my trunk and hand them out to most people I meet. I recommend it to nearly everyone. *From The Garden to the City* successfully blends simplicity with depth, theology with cultural commentary, and historical reflection with future thinking. It is the perfect first read for anyone looking for a biblical grounding in technology. This second edition is needed now more than ever before!"

—**James Kelly**, founder of FaithTech

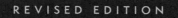

REVISED EDITION

FROM THE GARDEN TO THE CITY

The Place of Technology in the Story of God

John Dyer

KREGEL
PUBLICATIONS

From the Garden to the City: The Place of Technology in the Story of God
© 2011 by John Dyer
Second edition 2022

Published by Kregel Publications, a division of Kregel Inc., 2450 Oak Industrial
Dr. NE, Grand Rapids, MI 49505. www.kregel.com.

Cataloging-in-Publication Data is available from the Library of Congress.

ISBN 978-0-8254-3312-2, print
ISBN 978-0-8254-7806-2, epub
ISBN 978-0-8254-6953-4, Kindle

Printed in the United States of America

22 23 24 25 26 27 28 29 30 31 / 5 4 3 2 1

To Amber,
who taught me
Heidegger, laughter, and
unmediated love

CONTENTS

FOREWORD

JOHN DYER HAS WRITTEN a book that few could write. Trained both in information technology and in theology, and well versed in media ecology, he is unusually qualified to raise questions about how we make tools and how tools make us, focusing especially on the more recent developments in electronic and image-based technologies. With his distinctive background, Dyer is able to ask and answer two questions of our tools and technologies: What do they do for us? And, What do they do to us?

Dyer's viewpoint is self-consciously Christian without being reactionary, tech-savvy without being naive, and well considered without being pedantic. At a moment in history when our tools are being developed at a rate faster than our capacity to evaluate their impact, we need reliable guides to help us understand them well, so that we can use them thoughtfully and intentionally. John Dyer is such a guide, and this insightful volume dodges none of the difficult questions, while retaining a balanced and judicious consideration of those areas that do not yet enjoy universal consensus.

From the Garden to the City traces the history of technology and toolmaking and candidly acknowledges that both human wisdom and folly, both piety and impiety, both humility and pride, have contributed chapters to this complicated history. Neither technophobes nor technophiles will be entirely satisfied with either Dyer's judicious reasoning or his cautionary encouragements. Each will prefer total, apocalyptic warfare, and each will be uncomfortable with his sniper-like precision.

I have looked for a volume like this since I began teaching an Introduction to Media Ecology class in the early 2000s, and I commend it to all who are interested in electronic and image-based technologies, and to all whose thinking (like mine) has been influenced by people such as Walter Lippmann, Jacques Ellul, Marshall McLuhan, Daniel Boorstin, Walter Ong, Neil Postman, Winifred Gallagher, Maggie Jackson, Maryanne Wolf, Mark Bauerlein, William Powers, and Nicholas Carr.

For all those who desire to be wise and faithful followers of Christ without returning to his moment in technological history, this will prove to be a valuable, if not cherished, guide.

Dr. T. David Gordon
Professor of Religion and Greek
Grove City College
Grove City, PA

PREFACE TO THE SECOND EDITION

ONE OF THE PERILS of writing about technology is that it becomes dated before the file syncs to the cloud.

In the decade since the first edition of this book was published, our world has continued to accelerate technologically, with once-futuristic technology becoming mainstream (cryptocurrency, virtual reality, smart speakers, self-driving electric cars) and mainstream technology becoming commonplace (phones, social media, videoconferencing). Even with all this change, the core argument of the book—that theologically, technology is a good gift from God that plays a significant part in the biblical story; and that practically, technology is never neutral but has an embedded value system that transforms individuals and communities—is still true. And yet these technological accelerations and cultural movements invite updated examples and new reflection.

In the category of technology that has become commonplace, perhaps the most life-altering has been the way phones have come to saturate our lives. In 2010, we still called them "smartphones," and they were only just transitioning from the toys of the tech elite into the ubiquitous, ever-present, always-on glowing rectangles that permeate our lives. Our phones make incredible things possible, both good and bad, but they are significant not just because of what we can do with them but because of how we have rearranged our lives around them. We wake up to their alarms, respond to their notifications, record our most (in)significant moments with their cameras, and then scroll through their feeds as we fall asleep. Phones not only have reshaped our individual habits but they have also made larger societal shifts possible, such as enabling developing countries to skip wired phone and internet connections altogether, empowering "remix culture" where individuals collect and arrange values and beliefs to their tastes, and empowering companies like Uber to transform the transportation industry and Spotify to disrupt the music industry.

The ubiquity of phones, in turn, accelerated the use of social media, which was just emerging from college culture (Facebook) and Silicon Valley (Twitter) in the early 2010s. New platforms have come and gone (remember Google+?), and different demographic groups gravitate toward some platforms more than others, but social media is now a part of everything from schools and churches to politics and medicine. As with phones, the list of good and bad uses of social media is endless, but underlying that are profound changes to society, including political elections that centered on the use and abuse of social media, the rise of misinformation campaigns that accelerated an erosion of trust in traditional societal structures, and heightened tensions around important issues of justice and human rights.

The pandemic and lockdowns of 2020 and later only accelerated these technological changes, and people around the world embraced and adapted to digital technology literally overnight. The idea of online church was a mere footnote in the first edition of this book, but due to the pandemic it became something nearly every religious person in the world had experienced, along with online school, remote work, and grocery delivery. It is difficult to imagine how things would have played out if the pandemic had taken place twenty years earlier, when the internet was still young and tools like livestreaming and videoconferencing were not yet widely available. Today it is difficult to imagine life, relationships, and business without them.

As we have experienced the accelerations of mainstream technology becoming commonplace, we have also become more aware of the technology that was just coming on the market in 2010. For example, Bitcoin was invented in 2009, but it took years for it and its crypto-competitors to make their way into mainstream financial discussions. Virtual reality (VR), too, has been around for decades but has recently gone from being an expensive experimental technology to something that costs less than a phone to try and is now the focus of many companies, like Facebook's parent company, Meta. Talk of robots and artificial intelligence (AI) has also entered the mainstream, where AI can be loosely defined as anything we used to think only humans could do. This includes deepfake videos, self-driving cars, and medical diagnoses, and will expand to more in the years to come. As we talk to our smart speakers, ideas about the singularity, transhumanism, bioethics, and designer babies have also emerged from science fiction into podcast discussion points and everyday conversations.

Each of these events and trends are worthy of deep engagement and thoughtful discussion, though I can't fully address them all in an update to this book. But I have attempted to bring the examples and references throughout this edition into conversation with these events, while continuing to argue both that technology is still a good part of our image-bearing creativity and that, more than ever, we need godly wisdom developed in community to faithfully navigate this new world. I hope these updates will allow us to faithfully and soberly embrace technology as one of God's many good gifts.

ACKNOWLEDGMENTS

FOR GETTING THIS BOOK off the ground, I'd like to thank my college room-mate Frank Barnett, who encouraged me to start a blog after I emailed him a few thoughts about technology in the early 2000s. This eventually led me to the 2009 BibleTech Conference, where I gave a talk that Justin Taylor posted on his blog and that Ed Komoszewski from Kregel encouraged me to turn into this book. Thanks to them and God for such a providential turn of events.

While writing, numerous friends offered their encouragement, including my longtime friend Dave Furman, who somehow manages to be rather immediate even half a world away. Thanks also to the men in my small group, each of whom contributed something to this work: Barry Jones (culture), Jeff Taylor (music), Trey Hill (images), Josh Weise (typography), Brady Black (faith), Christian Hemberger (presence), and Dale Dunns (advocacy). Thanks is due to my writing and blogging friends both near and far: Matthew Lee Anderson, Rhett Smith, Scott McClellan, John Saddington, Tim Challies, and the rest. Thanks also to Dallas Theological

Seminary, which gave me a wonderful biblical education, and to my boss, Mark Yarbrough, who gave me time to write this book.

A special word of thanks is due to Dr. Albert Borgmann and Dr. T. David Gordon, both of whom allowed me to ask them questions as I wrote and whose work has been enormously helpful to me and others. I am indebted to those who took the time to read early versions of this book and offered helpful feedback, especially Adam Keiper of the *New Atlantis*. Since the first edition of this book, scholars such as Heidi Campbell, Tim Hutchings, Stephen Garner, Pete Phillips, and Mathew Guest have deepened my understanding of these areas beyond what I can share in these pages. Special thanks are due to members of the FaithTech Silicon Valley group who read an early version of the second edition and provided valuable input and feedback.

I am grateful for a wonderful family, including my mother, who raised me to be a person hopefully capable of writing a book someone (other than her) would read, and my father, who bought that first Apple IIe. To my dear sister, Ruthie, and my trusted brothers, David and Stephen: I hope our children are blessed with siblings as wonderful as you.

My children were just toddlers when this book was first published, and since then I've had the incredible joy of watching them grow and see the world with fresh wonder. They have shown me things about God's creation, human creativity, and the Father's love, for which I am eternally grateful.

And to my lovely, brilliant wife, Amber, thank you for waiting. Are you free Friday night?

INTRODUCTION

ONE DAY, A GUEST speaker brought an interesting contraption to our church. As our pastor introduced him, he pulled an old reel-to-reel movie projector out of its case and began to set it up. Some of the audience seemed to wonder why he'd bring something so technologically backward, but I was mesmerized as he attached the reels and weaved the celluloid film through a half-dozen channels and pulleys. After working with it for some time, he finally connected the film to the second reel, plugged it in, and flipped the switch, but then . . . click, click, click, click . . .

Nothing happened. Something was obviously wrong.

As the clicking sound continued, the room started to grow a little tense. People shifted awkwardly in their seats, letting our guest know he was wasting their time.

But not me. I wasn't bored at all, because I could see exactly what had gone wrong.

So I got up from my chair and marched straight down the aisle of the church, past the guest speaker, and up to the ancient, malfunctioning device.

Without saying a word, I began to undo his work and carefully rethread the film back through the correct channels.

The audience watched with some surprise, apparently aware that I had never used this device before. Some shook their heads in disbelief, while others shot knowing grins at each other. I continued to work, slowly threading the film, then reattached it to the second reel. I checked the plug, flipped a few switches, and then pressed the power button . . . whiiiirrrr . . . it worked!

Now, this story probably seems fairly ordinary. Tech people like me are always fixing things in churches. However, you might be interested to know that I have absolutely no memory of the events I've just described. The only reason I know it happened is that while I was growing up, whenever my mom met someone new, she liked to tell the story of how her three-year-old son had fixed a film projector he had never seen before.

And so began my love and fascination with all things technological, from mechanical projectors to radio control cars and planes to computers and mobile devices. I was the kind of kid who asked for a chemistry set for Christmas so I could do experiments in the garage, and who saved up money for an electronics kit from RadioShack so I could wire up an alarm for my bedroom. Of course, like most children of the '80s, I played countless hours of video games, but when I finally bought an Xbox, it was not so much because I wanted to play Xbox games but because I wanted to solder in a modchip and play around with home-brew software.

Fast-forward a few decades. As a young adult, I found that I loved doing two things. The first was teaching the Bible, which led me to attend seminary. The second was computer programming, which led me to work in the web development world. God graciously provided me a web design job at the seminary I was attending, allowing me to combine my love for God and his church with my love for technology.

As exciting as it was to do technology work for a ministry, I soon found that working for a ministry does not always pay all the bills. So I took on a few side projects that allowed me to build tools for companies like Apple, Microsoft, Harley-Davidson, Anheuser-Busch, the US Department of Defense, and Dallas's NPR affiliate.

Throughout my years in seminary, I continued to study and work hard in both theological studies and programming. I spent as much time learning Greek and Hebrew as I did learning languages like PHP, C#, Swift, Python, HTML, and JavaScript.

But in my final semester of seminary, a professor who was known for both his brilliance and his shocking, out-of-nowhere statements said something that changed everything for me. In the middle of a lecture addressing a variety of current issues in society and culture, he looked straight at all of us and said, "One of the most dangerous things you can believe in this world is that technology is neutral."

Wait, what? I thought. Surely he must have misspoken.

After all, nothing could be more obvious than the fact that technology is neutral. All that matters is *how* we use it. Right?

As he kept talking, I started arguing with the professor in my head. I could not think of a single tool, device, or technology that was morally good or evil in and of itself. Yes, a tool like the nuclear bomb has been used to kill hundreds of thousands of people, but it is based on technology that can also be used to generate inexpensive electricity for millions of people.

Sure, people can choose to abuse computers and the internet, using them for all kinds of illicit purposes, from identity theft to the distribution of pornography. But the reason I chose web development for an occupation was that I also knew the internet could be used for incredible good too. Outside work hours, I built websites like biblewebapp.com and bestcommentaries .com to help church leaders find good biblical resources. My entire goal was to use the latest and greatest technology for the good of Christ and his church.

What could be so dangerous about that?

I returned to class the next day prepared to ask the professor about his statement, armed with the best arguments I could muster about why technology was, in fact, neutral. However, when I arrived that day, the professor was not there. He had fallen ill and would not be able to return to class that semester.

What was I to do? How could I be sure I was right? And what if the professor was right after all? What if there was some problem with technology I had never considered? Does the Bible actually say anything about technology? Can we say anything more profound or helpful about our technological world than simply, "Don't be evil" (Google's old corporate motto)?

So I headed straight for my computer and started scouring the internet for resources. Strangely, though, when I attempted to find specifically Christian reflections on technology, I found very little. A quick search for "theology and technology" turned up dozens of results on how to *use* technology. But beyond calls to "redeem technology" or use social media less often, I found very little about how technology fits into the biblical story.

Just as I was about to give up in frustration, a dear friend who worked two floors up from my office gave me a book on Marshall McLuhan's thought, and another friend who lived halfway around the world gave me a book by Neil Postman, a student of McLuhan. I later found out that McLuhan and Postman founded an academic discipline called media ecology, which studies how technology operates within cultures and how it changes them over time. Media ecologists look at what happens when a technology enters a culture, the same way that a biologist examines what happens when a new animal species enters an ecological environment.

Digging a bit more, I found a subdiscipline of philosophy called— obviously enough—philosophy of technology, which asks questions about the nature of technology and how it relates to what it means to be human. These questions include "Does technology have an independent nature?" and "Should humans be classified as 'tool-making animals'?" More recently, from the field of sociology, a new discipline of digital religion has emerged, which takes a more data-driven approach to understanding how media and technology affect religious behavior and practices. Scholars in this field put the theories of those above to the test and see how regular people understand God and faith in a technological world.

Some of these writers made me worry about where technology has taken us and lament the damage we do to one another with it, while others made me appreciate human ingenuity and creativity all the more. As I began to reread the biblical story with technology in mind, I saw things I hadn't noticed before about how deeply God cares about the things we make and how we use them. God's original calling on humanity was to have dominion over all the earth, making things from what he had made, moving humanity, as the title of this book suggests, from the garden to the city, or more specifically from the garden of Eden (Gen. 2) to the city from heaven (Heb. 11:16; Rev. 21). This book is my attempt to connect the story of Scripture with the world of both ancient and modern technology, so we can fulfill our role as God's image bearers in a digital age.

The argument I will make in this book might seem counterintuitive. As we will see in a following chapter, most people assume that technology is simply neutral, and that all that matters is how we use it. I plan to upend this notion with two key ideas. First, as we study the Scriptures, we will find that, theologically speaking, technology is a God-given *good*. And second, we will discover that, practically speaking, technology is *never neutral*.

By saying technology is good, I don't mean that every *use* of technology is good, nor do I mean that every individual tool or device is good. What I mean is that God created humans to bear his image, and one aspect of this is our creative capacity, which includes making and using technology. It's true that any technology can be used for good or evil, but its fundamental nature is tied back to image-bearing humanity, which God has declared as "good."

So if technology can be used for good or bad, doesn't that mean it's neutral? I will argue no; technology is never neutral. Whenever we use tools, from shovels and books to phones and virtual reality, regardless of whether we use them for good or evil, the act of using them forms us physically, mentally, spiritually, and relationally. The problem with thinking of technology as neutral is that doing so often makes us miss all the other non-neutral ways its presence in our lives affects us. For example, if someone were to argue that online giving is neutral (i.e., it can be directed to good organizations or bad ones), I might point out that the act of giving in an offering plate, which requires prior planning and often happens in front of people, is a very different experience of worship than setting up a recurring transaction. While the content in both forms of giving is the same (money), and both are good and God-honoring, there are non-neutral differences between the two that disciple us in distinct ways and alter how we relate to ourselves, our community, and even God.

Our goal then is not simply to condemn technology as bad, neither is it to naively embrace every new gadget. Nor is it to glibly assume that because we are using a tool for good ends, nothing else matters. Instead, we are to carefully examine each new tool, device, and service, noticing the goodness of God in giving us such powers, and yet asking ourselves not only how we can use it but also how using it might transform us in the process.

As I did with the film projector so many years ago, I will use the following pages to dismantle the concept of technology, examine it carefully, and then put it back together again. My goal is to retell the story of technology in a way that honors God and the reason he put us here on earth.

QUESTIONS

- What is your first memory of a new technology, one that wasn't around when you were born? What was different about it compared to what came before?
- How do you see your faith informing or being informed by the way you create and use technology?
- What resources (books, websites, podcasts, people) have been helpful to you in thinking about technology?

1

PERSPECTIVE

Just down the street from my house, there is a little Indian market my family and I like to visit when we need to pick up a few items for dinner. On the short walk there, we'll pass the neighbors from Korea who own a liquor store, the retired Germans with the meticulously kept lawn, a Chinese real estate agent who named both his dog and his daughter after himself, a tall Bulgarian man and his wife who both work on the chips that power our phones' internet connection, the chief ice-cream scientist for an Italian gelato company, an Egyptian friend who brings the most delicious treats for Eid al-Fitr, and an elderly black woman still displaced from Hurricane Katrina.

Some of these neighbors live in expensive homes, send their kids to expensive private schools, and drive new luxury vehicles. Just a few blocks away, however, another set of neighbors can barely afford their low-income, government-subsidized housing. They send their kids to public schools, travel by public transportation, and wear clothing from Goodwill.

Dotting the surrounding area are churches, mosques, temples, and synagogues, each serving the unique religious needs of our community.

Scattered among these places of worship are dozens of restaurants serving every kind of cultural and ethnic food one can imagine. At the center of it all is Walmart, that "placeless place" where we all go to find what we need.

On the surface, my neighborhood would seem to be fairly diverse and cosmopolitan. We are made up of people of different religions, genders, ages, occupations, food preferences, cultures, income levels, and native languages. And yet, for all our very real differences, my neighbors and I have something in common that transcends those differences and orders nearly every part of our lives. It's obviously not our ethnic heritage nor our common upbringing. It's not the place we live nor our hatred of the August heat in Texas.

The one thing we all share in common is a lifestyle thoroughly saturated with technology.

A Completely Different World

When people use the word *technology*, most of the time they mean something like "internet-connected gadgets" or apps of some kind. Computer scientist Alan Kay (inventor of the mouse) famously picked up on our tendency to think of technology as the latest thing by defining technology as "anything that was invented after you were born."[1] He was pointing out how quickly we take for granted technology that once seemed amazing but now feels commonplace.

If we broaden our perspective on technology to consider more than just the last several decades, we can see just how rapidly our world has been changing. A century ago, the idea of communicating electronically with anyone at any time would have seemed like magic. By the standards of 1900, the differences between communicating via landline, Zoom, or virtual reality would be meaningless, because a person from that era would not yet be accustomed to hearing disembodied voices from across the globe. Even the most educated and advanced individual of the early 1800s could not see a distinction between the clunky big-screen TVs of the 1980s (that took up an entire living room) and a modern home theater, because they lived in the time before even photography was commonplace.

Almost all the tools we use on a daily basis—light bulbs, cars, washing machines, air-conditioning, TVs, phones, the internet, and so on—were invented in the past 150 years, but these tools are so normal to us that it seems strange to call them technology.

Technology has changed our world so drastically that the biblical character Abraham of 2000 BC would probably have more in common with Abraham Lincoln of the early 1800s than Lincoln would have with us in the twenty-first century. The biblical Abraham's father raised cattle, and Mr. Lincoln planted pumpkins, but most of us spend the majority of our time indoors, working at desks with little knowledge of the natural world. Both men attended small religious gatherings with people they knew well from the surrounding area, while we drive several miles to sit next to people we often don't know (or we join services online with people halfway around the world). They lived in small, one-bedroom dwellings lit by candles; we live in comparatively enormous homes equipped with electricity and internet connections. They wrote letters and spoke in person; we write electronically and speak through devices. They weathered the seasons; we control the weather with air-conditioning that contributes to global climate change.

We could go on making various comparisons, but the point is that our world is so uniformly technological that even in an ethnically and religiously diverse community like my neighborhood, the day-to-day activities of my neighbors probably have more in common with one another than with the founders of our country. Technology has become a kind of supra-cultural phenomenon that finds its way into every aspect of our diverse lives. Not a single one of these devices or behaviors existed just over a century ago, and yet all of us treat them as if they were as normal as the water we drink or the air we breathe.

So why does any of this matter? If more advanced technology leads to things like increased quality of life and faster ways to spread the gospel, what could be the harm in any of it? Why do we need to pay close attention to the influence of technology? The story of a certain young pastor and yet another projector shows what can happen when we ignore technology.

The Youth Pastor and the Projector

After I graduated from college, I took a job as a youth pastor at a nearby church. One of my first requests to the church was to buy a video projector for our youth room. As a youth pastor at a *Bible* church, my job was to make sure the kids were firmly planted in the Scriptures. That meant that they needed to regularly encounter the words of the Bible with their own eyes. The only problem was that many of the kids didn't bring Bibles. I figured that a projector would allow me to put the words of God on-screen so everyone could read together whether they brought a Bible or not. (And as a bonus, we could play video games on a gigantic screen and call it "ministry.")

Eventually, a generous church member donated a projector, and I immediately began using it during all my teaching. I made fantastic sermon outlines and highlighted important words in the text. I peppered my teaching with captivating stories and concluded them with hilarious punch lines. I taught verse by verse, but I also made the Scriptures relevant and applicable to the kids' lives. They seemed to eat it up, and at the risk of sounding haughty, I think I was a pretty good youth leader.

But then things started to go terribly wrong.

I noticed that fewer and fewer kids were bringing their Bibles to church each week. And those who did bring them rarely opened them when I was teaching. Perhaps I was not the model youth pastor I thought myself to be.

I tried saying, "Open your Bibles to . . ." more often, but that didn't seem to help—they just ignored me when I said it. I tried toning down my wit and charm and focusing more on the text of Scripture, but no matter how much I emphasized the Bible, the kids still wouldn't bring or open theirs. Finally, I pulled aside one of my students and said, "I talk to y'all all the time about how important the Bible is, but I notice you don't bring your Bible to church anymore. Why don't you think the Bible is important?"

She answered, "But I *do* think the Bible is important! I just like reading it on the screen with everybody else. Why would I bring a Bible if you project it on-screen?"

This situation opened my eyes to how the technologies that surround us can have an impact on something as intimate as how we encounter the

Scriptures. I imagined that the projector would level the playing field and give everyone equal access to the Word of God. In my mind, a projector was a perfectly normal thing to bring into a church. All I was doing was taking the unchanging, eternal Word of God and transferring it to a newer, better medium that had the power to reach more students. I never considered that the projector would profoundly transform the way my students encountered God's Word and each other.

I didn't fully understand what had happened that day, but years later, when I began to study the effects technology can have on people, I initially felt like I had acted with terrible ignorance. I wondered, How could I have done so much damage to my kids without even knowing it? My technological choices meant that suburban American kids—*gasp!*—weren't bringing their Bibles into church buildings. After all, what's a Bible church without Bibles?

However, as I contemplated this, I realized that my perspective was even more myopic than I had first thought. Whereas I initially considered not bringing a Bible to church a tragedy, I soon realized that is a relatively recent phenomenon in church history. Until the printing press made Bibles inexpensive and available to everyone, individuals rarely owned their own copy of the Bible. Every single believer from Moses to Martin Luther—from 1500 BC to AD 1500—encountered God's Word by going to church and *listening* to it alongside others. They almost never had the chance to *read* the Bible for themselves. This meant that for nearly three thousand years, there was not a single believer in the one true God who ever had a "quiet time" as we know it today. Only rabbis and priests had access to handwritten copies of the Bible, but common people simply could not afford them. Gutenberg's printing press allowed families to purchase a copy of the Scriptures, but it was not until the twentieth century that it became common for individuals to own a personal copy of the Bible.

Looking back on what happened in my youth pastor days, I realize the projector had actually allowed my kids to experience God's Word in a way that might be closer to the pre–printing press era. My students had given up their individualized Bible with custom covers and specialized study notes and had begun reading the same words on the same screen together, as a community of faith. By transitioning from print to projector, we had moved forward technologically and yet backward culturally. Today, most of us have Bible apps on our phones, shifting the medium and the expectations around it yet again. It's possible that someone who only uses apps might not have a good grasp of how the Bible is laid out or how much larger the Old Testament is than the New Testament. More significantly, research suggests that people interpret passages differently on a phone than they do in print.[2]

It turns out that these kinds of cultural shifts have been well documented by historians of technology. Some even argue that the last five hundred years—from the time of the printing press to the time of the smartphone—will be seen as an aberration in human history.[3] These five centuries will have been the only time in human history when printed text was the dominant form of communication. Today, with smartphones, video chat, and VR, we are returning to a culture of spoken words rather than printed text, and yet those spoken words are not shared with people who are physically nearby.

My point here is not to argue that it is better to hear the Bible orally than to read it in print, or that reading on a screen with a group is better than either of those. Instead, it is important to recognize how little attention we pay to the technologies we use to encounter the Word of God. While God's words are eternal and unchanging, when we change the tools we use to access those words, the new medium brings subtle changes to our practices of worship, interpretation, and community. When we fail to recognize the impact of such technological change, we run the risk of allowing our tools to dictate our methods and disciple our people. Technology should not dictate our values or our methods. Rather, we must use technology *out of* our convictions and values.

When I installed the projector, I still mistakenly believed that technology was simply neutral, and all that mattered was how I used it. I thought that as long as I used the projector for good things like showing the Bible and avoided bad things like R-rated movies (or some 1980s PG movies), I was operating in a distinctly Christian way. What I didn't realize at the time was that technology is never neutral because it has a shaping power on us and those around us. Whether we use it for good or evil, every technology has a set of values that intersects with our own, and we must learn together to see and discern those values so we can use technology critically and faithfully.

The Myth of Technology

So why is it that we tend not to recognize the changes that technology brings? Why did I have so little awareness of how the printed Bible had shaped my expectation of church and how the projected Bible would reshape it?

Neil Postman attempted to explain this by saying that over time "technology tends to become mythic."[4] By *myth*, Postman wasn't referring to a legend or fantasy story. Instead, he used the word *myth* to describe the way of life that people think of as normal. In this sense, a myth is the story that develops over time about how the world works and what makes sense to a group of people. For example, most people know that leaders of the United States are chosen by voting. Before July 4, 1776, the idea of voting for leaders was new and radical, but over time voting has become a part of our shared myth about the way government is supposed to work.

When a new technology comes along, it too seems strange, out of place, and even magical. As sci-fi writer Arthur C. Clarke once quipped, "Any sufficiently advanced technology is indistinguishable from magic."[5] Sitting in a coffee shop, the person with the brand-new laptop—a little slimmer and lighter than last year's model—stands out. However, as futurist Jamais Cascio writes, "As [technologies] move from the pages of a science fiction story to the pages of a catalog, something interesting happens: they lose their power to disturb. They're no longer the advance forces of the techpocalypse, they're the latest manifestation of the fashionable, the ubiquitous, and the banal. They're normal."[6]

Today nearly every adult in the United States has a phone. But in the late 1990s, even a "cell phone" was considered a bit of an extravagance, only for very important businesspeople. Going back in time, the same could be said of portable music players (the first Sony Walkman was released in 1979), microwaves (1947), air-conditioning (1920s), and human flight (1903). Each technology was a revolution when it first arrived, but now they are all such a part of everyday life that it's difficult to imagine life without them.

The longer a particular practice or device has been around, the more solidly mythic it becomes in our culture. Eventually we stop thinking about why it was there in the first place, and over time we lose the ability—or desire—to question its presence. Those who might question a common technology—like phones or microwaves—might as well be crazy! It would be like doubting that hot dogs should be eaten at sporting events or that Texans should have air-conditioning.

Adding to this, each generation tends to approach technology from a slightly different perspective. Douglas Adams, author of *The Hitchhiker's Guide to the Galaxy*, once grouped technology into three categories. First, echoing Alan Kay, "everything that's already in the world when you're born is just normal." Then, "anything that gets invented between then and before you turn thirty is incredibly exciting and creative and with any luck you can make a career out of it." Finally, "anything that gets invented after you're thirty is against the natural order of things and the beginning of the end of civilisation as we know it until it's been around for about ten years when it gradually turns out to be alright really."[7] In other words, each generation is equipped with a different myth concerning technology. The faster technology develops and the less perspective we have, the more stratified our myths become. Similarly, different cultural groups tend to negotiate technological change differently depending on how its values intersect with those of their community.

Shortsighted Critiques of Technology

These generational gaps mean that younger people often uncritically embrace any and all technology while older generations sometimes make shortsighted critiques of technology. Consider, for example, a *New York Times* article discussing how preteen children interact online and via text messaging. The author begins by describing how teens chat through various apps late into the night, and her tone suggests that she disapproves of this way of interacting through technology. She then laments, "Children used to actually talk to their friends. Those hours spent on the family princess phone or hanging out with pals in the neighborhood after school vanished long ago."[8]

The author obviously wants to contrast the technological communication her children engage in with the embodied, face-to-face encounters she remembers from her youth. But did you notice how she paired "hanging out with pals in the neighborhood after school" with "hours spent on the [landline] phone" as if both were equally non-technological?

Chances are the author was born after the telephone was invented and turned thirty sometime before texting or social media. For her, talking on the phone feels natural or even "real" while app-based communication does not. But I imagine that if we were to dig deeply into the *New York Times* archives, we might find a similar article written in the 1950s that would criticize "talking for hours on the phone." Just a generation ago, talking on the phone for hours would have seemed as foreign and unhealthy as the texting habits of today's children. If we were to dig even further back in the archives, a pattern would quickly emerge in which the older generation is worried about the technology of the new generation, while they are largely unaware of their own technological heritage. How can we question the next generation's technology if we don't even understand our own?

It turns out that the phenomenon of questioning new technology while clinging to older technology is not limited to *New York Times* authors and youth pastors like myself. It happens at all levels of society and in churches around the world.

Uncovering the Myth

What this tells us is that the way we talk about and understand technology is in some ways dictated by where we sit along the timeline of technological progress. Rather than taking our cues about technology from the Scriptures and the outline of God's plan for humanity, we seem to be locked in a cycle of questioning the really, really new but accepting the just barely old. We question the young for the blind acceptance of the latest gadgets, but we do so driving our computerized cars to and from church sipping on coffee grown on another continent.

Today's technology has the power to heal the sick and make the blind see (Luke 7:22), yet it also has the power to overwhelm us and distract us from what is truly important. When technology has distracted us to the point that we no longer examine it, it gains the greatest opportunity to enslave us.

To avoid this cycle, we'll need to start from the beginning and explore how the Scriptures treat technology. In the coming chapters, we will follow the outline of the biblical story, beginning with creation and continuing to the fall and to redemption and finally to restoration.

As we discover the role of technology in each chapter of the biblical story, it will lead us to a follow-up question in the following chapter that will help us better understand technology. Chapter 2 will introduce the relationship of stories, faith, and technology, showing how they interact to form our ideas about the world. In chapter 3, we will delve into the biblical story starting with the creation, where God gives humanity the role of reflecting his image and charges them with cultivating and keeping the garden. In the following chapter, we will explore the unique role of technology among the things humans create. Then in chapter 5, we will look at Adam and Eve's rebellion (the fall) and the subsequent evil uses of technology that find their origin in Cain and his family. This will lead us to explore a more fully developed philosophical approach to technology in chapter 6. In chapter 7, we will begin exploring the various mediums[9] through which God accomplishes his plan of redemption, and in chapter 8 we will see how those mediums operate within a culture and how they shape individuals. In chapter 9, we will complete the biblical story by looking at what God will do when he restores the earth. Chapter 10 will pick up where the biblical story leaves off, examining how the world of technology has continued to develop into a kind of religion unto itself. Finally, in chapter 11 we will look at the digital revolution and use what we've learned to help us understand and live faithfully in our current age and with the advances to come.

At one end of this story is a pristine garden prepared by God for humankind to develop and transform. At the other end is a glorious, heavenly city full of human creations, art, and technology. At the center is our Savior Jesus Christ crucified on a cross, the most horrific of all technological distortions, built by transforming a tree from the natural world into a tool of death. Yet in his resurrection, Christ redeemed even that tool, transforming it into the symbol of our faith that eternally portrays his power over death and sin.

In the time between the garden and the city, between Christ's first and second coming (when he will complete his work of redemption and restoration), we must work diligently to understand how to live faithfully in this technology-saturated world. To help us better understand our world, we will combine what we find in the Scriptures with insights from some of the best thinkers on technology, theology, and culture. We will largely limit our discussion to "everyday" kinds of technology, meaning that we won't spend significant time addressing important societal issues like health care, nuclear weapons, or biotechnology,[10] but the overall ethics we find in Scripture can apply broadly to all areas of human making.

Embracing Technology Faithfully

It would be convenient if we could simply label every technology as either good (use it as much as you want) or bad (never, ever use it). But Arthur Boers posits that technology is more like the yellow light on a traffic signal.[11] Unlike green, which always means go, or red, which always means stop, the yellow light is a call for a discerning look at the entire situation. Technology is a God-given good part of what it means to be human, but first we need to recognize that, like all of creation, it was warped by the fall; and second, we must learn to detect how it shapes us even as we use it.

A surprisingly helpful example of this kind of technological discernment can be found in an obscure passage in one of John's letters. In 2 John 1:12, the apostle wrote: "I have much to write to you, but I do not want to use paper and ink. Instead, I hope to visit you and talk with you face to face, so that our joy may be complete." For John and the early church, pen and ink was the primary communication technology they had to choose from and evaluate. Though writing might seem low tech to us today, the philosophers of that day were considering how it was influencing learning and community.

A few hundred years before John wrote his letters, the Greek philosopher

Socrates expressed concern about the technology of writing. He believed that learning through dialogue was the key to helping people grow in wisdom, and he worried that writing would make people knowledgeable, but it would fail to make them wise. Socrates was so worried about the damage that writing could cause that he never wrote any of his own ideas down.[12]

In his letters, John gives us a model of how to consider the advantages and disadvantages of a particular technology. Notice that he says there are some things he would rather not write and would prefer to reserve for when he could come to them face-to-face. We could read this as John saying face-to-face is always better than technologically mediated communication. But John isn't being critical of writing or saying that he was using it only as a last resort. Rather, he is telling us that both are valuable for the health of the church, we just need to have the discernment to know when to use which form. After all, if the apostles didn't embrace the technology of writing, we wouldn't have the New Testament (and John wouldn't have been able to brag about being a faster runner than Peter in John 20:4). And yet, he also recognizes that certain things are best handled in person. In the internet era, we sometimes talk about "online" and "offline" as two entirely different things, where one is real and the other is less than real. But researchers like Heidi Campbell[13] have shown that we move fluidly between online and offline contexts several times throughout the day, using online communication to plan and enrich our offline encounters.

Our goal, then, is not to say which technology is superior, but to develop the discernment to know which form is best for which activity, which medium for which message. The apostle Paul, for example, often expressed a deep longing to see his faraway friends (Rom. 1:11), but in other cases he felt writing a letter would be more redemptive (1 Cor. 4:14–21; 2 Cor. 7:8–9). If we take the time to understand how each communication technology works and what it values, we can use them alongside our face-to-face conversation in a way that, as John says, makes our joy complete.

The apostles appear to have been aware of the strengths and weaknesses of the new technology of writing, and they made calculated choices about when to use it in service of the embodied life of the church and for the flourishing of their city. In doing so, they honored our Lord and built up his body.

My hope is that in the coming chapters we can learn to do the same with today's technology.

QUESTIONS

- How do you tend to think of technology? Is it primarily good, bad, or neutral?
- What is a technology that has come along in your lifetime that has had a major impact on your world and the world around you?
- What are some technologies that you use regularly but rarely think about (i.e., have become unquestioned or "mythic")?

2

IMAGINATION

When I was in first grade, one of my parents' friends from Mississippi gave us a huge wooden fort. The fort was over twenty feet tall, with a ladder reaching up into the main platform and a pole sliding back down for quick escapes. For my siblings and me, the fort was the perfect opportunity for our young imaginations to run wild. That fort transformed us into pirates at sea, doctors saving patients, and knights storming the castle.

It's commonly held that adults have lost the propensity for the imaginative play that my siblings and I took for granted. Kids, we are told, have the ability to look past the world as it is and see the world as it could be, but adults are only able to see the real world. Yet when it comes to using technology, the ability to imagine and tell stories is constantly being awakened even in adults. In fact, whenever we use a tool, whether it be a shovel or a phone, three powerful stories unfold: how we shape the world with technology, how technology shapes us, and how we see the world through technology. Exploring these three stories in this chapter will help us begin to uncover the place of technology in our lives and in the story God is telling.

The First Story: Using Technology

The first story is about how humans shape the world using tools. This begins with the stories we tell ourselves when we see a new tool. As we imagine ourselves using it, we see in our mind's eye all the great new things we can accomplish with the device. Whether we come across a faster computer, an egg white separator, or a space shuttle, our minds attempt to understand the tool by imagining what it would be like to use it.

Historian of technology David Nye writes, "Composing a narrative and using a tool . . . each requires the imagination of altered circumstances. . . . In each case, one imagines how present circumstances might be made different."[1] Just as storytellers imagine new worlds for their books and movies, we too envision an alternate reality when we imagine how we'll use a tool. We see the world as it is, and then through the tool, we see the world as it could be.

Like little kids making their hands into the shapes of pistols and imagining what the world would be like if they were daring and important spies, adults imagine how the world might be better, faster, or cleaner if only we had a robotic vacuum cleaner, a four-wheel-drive vehicle, or a next generation phone. The mind of a child envisions a world of adventure and purpose while the mind of an adult longs for a world of comfort, ease, and power.

Not all of us, however, imagine the story the same way. Some look at new gadgets and think, "Wow, that would make my life so much easier." Others have the opposite reaction: "That's ridiculous," they say. "I would never need that thing." Different cultures and communities, too, assign different worth to new technology. However, even when the reactions are different, we are all imagining what it would be like to use the tool and basing our conclusions about the tool on how the story ends.

Though we might not realize it, we compose these mini-narratives whenever we encounter even the simplest gadget. If we happen to see a shovel, our minds can easily imagine the act of digging a hole, visualizing how the ground will look after we're finished. This small effort of the imagination has a clear movement from beginning (the world before the shovel) to middle (the act of digging) to end (the world with a new hole)—the basic arc of any story. It might not be a long story, or a particularly interesting one, but it's still a story, and when it's over, the world will be a different place.

But the stories we tell ourselves about tools have an important difference from the stories we read in books. As we read a story in a book, we are transported to an alternate world that the author has crafted from carefully chosen words. For a little while we inhabit that world and are possibly even transformed by it. Eventually, however, we must return to the real world, and we realize that those places and those people don't really exist.

Yet when we use technology, we are no longer constructing a fictional world using words. Instead, we are reconstructing the actual world using tools. Unlike tales of goblins or love at first sight, the stories we tell ourselves about technology can become everyday realities. If we imagine a world with a hole, a shovel can create that world for us. If we imagine a world free from headaches, medicine can make that a reality, and an AI just might find a new solution for us.

Technology, then, is the bridge from this world to the imagined one. From Adam's invention of clothing to Edison's invention of the light bulb, technology is the means by which we transport ourselves to the better worlds we are constantly imagining. The more powerful the tool, the more fully our visions can be realized. When we stumble into a problem we want to solve, we instinctively search for a tool that can help us get from the world with the problem to a world where the problem is solved.

If you're not yet convinced of the link between tools and our love of stories, you need only observe any advertisement in print, on TV, or online. In thirty seconds or less, advertisements tap into the basic movement from our present circumstances to a newer, better world. First, the commercial will call attention to a problem in our lives. Then it will promise a brighter, cleaner, and faster world made possible by the product on-screen. In fact, every single commercial we watch or hear has the basic plot structure of beginning (our current limited existence), middle (acquiring a shiny new tool), and end (a better world only available to those with the tool). Commercials for fast cars promise to transport the buyer to a thrilling world of speed and social status. Billboards for new shaving products promise the buyer a world free from the nicks and cuts offered by competitors. Keynotes for the latest device invite us to imagine "What will you do with Product X?"

The allure of technology, then, is a promise that with the right tools we can take this broken world and mold it into the better one we all desire. The transforming role of technology is evidenced in the way many scholars define technology. For example, Dutch engineering professor and theologian Egbert Schuurman writes, "We can say that we are talking about technology when we use tools to shape nature in the service of human ends."[2] David Mindell sees technology as the "constellation of tools, machinery, systems, and techniques that manipulate the natural world for human ends."[3]

These "human ends" they mention are the story we tell with technology, the means by which we transform the world as it is into the world we desire. What we often fail to notice, however, is that it is not only the world that gets transformed by technology. We too are transformed bodily, mentally, and even spiritually.

The Second Story: Technology Using Us

If the first story of technology is how we humans shape the world using tools, the second story is how those tools in turn shape us.

To see how this happens, let's again use the example of our trusty shovel. Imagine for a moment that we see an advertisement telling us how exciting our world could be with several holes in the ground. The advertisement convinces us that a shovel is the means by which we can get to the wonderful world of holes, and so we purchase the shovel and begin digging. After some time we put the shovel down, wipe our brow, and survey the work we have done. Proudly, we see that the world is quite different from what it was a few hours ago. We, dear friends, are now standing on holey ground.

But if we stop for a moment and look down at our hands, we'll see that they too have been changed by the shovel. They will be rubbed raw, exposing the first signs of the blisters that are sure to develop while we sleep.[4]

Over time, as we dig hole after hole, reshaping the world as we see fit, our hands, arms, and backs will be changed as well. Those blisters will turn into calluses, and our once weak arms will grow stronger and more muscular.

Our minds too will develop a sense of the land and how best to approach it. When the job is completed, the tool will have transformed both the creator and the creation. Indeed, as John Culkin, a student of Marshall McLuhan, wrote, "We shape our tools and thereafter our tools shape us."[5]

In this sense, technology sits between us and the world, changing and molding both at once. The world feels the spade, but we feel the handle. We use the tool to dig at the ground, but in another sense the ground uses the tool to chafe at our hands. The shovel connects us to the earth, but it also functions to insulate us from directly touching the soil. Our primary connection, then, is with the tool, not with the creation itself, giving the tool the opportunity to simultaneously shape both the world and its user.

But notice that the transformation technology brings happens regardless of *why* a person uses a tool. One person might use a shovel to break ground on a new orphanage, while another might use it to conceal stolen goods. Clearly, one is morally superior to the other, but the moral intent does not change the fact that both the righteous and the wicked end up with blistered hands and aching backs. This means that the moral purpose of digging does not change the way that the act of using a shovel transforms its user.

Though most of us don't realize it, any time we walk into a gym, we choose tools based on their ability to transform our bodies. There are tools to shape our arms, back, chest, and legs, and there are even tools that shape those parts of our bodies in different ways. A treadmill helps our legs become long and lean, while a leg press can make our quadriceps strong and powerful. The more we use one or the other, the more our body adapts and is shaped in a particular direction.

And while shovels and gym equipment mold us physically, newer technology can shape us mentally, spiritually, and socially as well. From radio to television to the internet, scientists and cultural critics have long contended that our communication and information technologies influence the way we think in the same way that shoes affect the way we run. Nicholas Carr argued in his book *The Shallows* that our brains work just like our muscles: when we perform a mental task repeatedly, our neural pathways rewire themselves to become better at that task.[6]

For example, people who spend long hours reading books with complex ideas tend to become good at that activity. Likewise, people who spend their days consuming small pieces of content on social media tend to have minds particularly suited to performing that task. But just as it is difficult to master both running long distances and lifting heavy weights with our legs, these two mental tasks are mutually exclusive to a degree. Those who have developed the ability to consume complex arguments in books tend to feel overwhelmed by the rush of data online, while those who do most of their reading online and on smaller mobile screens can see complex connections but tend to lose concentration when they attempt to focus on a single idea for long periods of time. For example, this book is around seventy thousand words, meaning an average reader should be able to finish it in around five hours. However, those who have developed the skill and habit of skimming and scrolling online may find it difficult to read a book for that duration.

Again, as with the blisters and calluses from a shovel, these mental transformations happen without reference to morality. Whether a person spends long periods of time reading Christian apologetics or atheist literature, the reader will increase his or her ability to understand complex arguments. And whether a person reads thousands of tweets from celebrity actors and musicians or from famous Christian authors and preachers, the skill of consuming massive amounts of small information bites will increase.

Of course, the content we consume is important, but often we focus so much on the content that we miss the importance of the medium through which we consume it. In fact, sometimes the effects of a medium are more important than any content transmitted through that medium.

Marshall McLuhan coined the now famous phrase "The medium is the message" to describe this phenomenon, writing, "This is merely to say that the personal and social consequences of any medium—that is, of any extension of ourselves—result from the new scale that is introduced into our affairs by each extension of ourselves or by any new technology."[7] What he meant was that the transformative effect of a technology is so powerful that it often overshadows what we say or do with that medium. So a treadmill would be the medium and its transformative message is increasing our ability to run. With the medium of Twitter, the message is increasing our ability to consume short, disconnected sentences. If we think of Amazon as a medium, its significance is not just about *what* we buy but about how our world is restructured when almost anything can be purchased with same-day shipping.

McLuhan's main interest was not the blisters individuals receive from the shovel but rather the social and cultural transformation that happens in a group of people who have shovels. When we use tools to transform the world into the one we imagine, everyone around us is forced to respond and adapt to those changes. For example, when music moved from physical media (records, tapes, and CDs) to digital downloads and streaming, we were transported to a world where music was easier to find and consume. But this technology also changed the relationships between bands, labels, producers, and consumers. It doesn't matter if we listen to classical music, Christian music, or music with explicit lyrics, the mediums of digital downloads and streaming music sends a "message" to us about the meaning and place of music in our lives and to the music industry about how to make money from the consumption of art.

This happens because technology is not only situated between us and the world but also between one human and another. Right now, this book functions as an interface between you and me. Through the technologies of language, writing, paper, ink, and ebooks, you have access to the thoughts I've written. Just as a shovel is an interface between the builder and the world, this book is a channel between writer and reader. In one sense, the book connects two minds previously disconnected. Yet at the same time it connects, the book also forms a wedge between two people. When one person is reading another's thoughts, those two people cannot be fully present to one other.

And so it is with phones, email, video chat, and all of the communication tools we use today. They both connect us and put something between us. Psalm 1 tells us that we are molded and shaped by the company we keep, but when we connect with people through technology, the medium becomes part of the mediating equation in how that molding and shaping takes place.

Today, this is further influenced by the companies that make our tools, some of whom are intentionally designing them to battle for our attention.

Technology has the power to transform the world into the one we imagine, but it also has the power to transform our bodies, our mental capabilities, and our relational worlds. But there is a third, even more powerful story that technology has to tell.

The Third Story: What It Means

The third and final story we tell with technology happens when all that transforming we do to the world and ourselves finds its way into our souls. We know that shovels transform the earth and reshape our hands, but—taking a step back—we must wonder why humans dig at all. Computers help us compute things, but what is the big question we are trying to answer? Cars take us from here to there, but where exactly are we going? In other words, why are we doing all of this technology, and how does it fit into what we believe about the purpose and meaning of life?

One obvious answer might be that we are trying to reduce suffering in the world, and thankfully technology has accomplished that to some degree. In 1850, the average life expectancy of someone living in North America or Europe was around thirty-eight years.[8] But today, the average life expectancy is well over seventy years. That means that in less than two centuries, technology advanced to a point where it doubled the length of our lives. Much of this increase is due to advances in obstetrics, which led to a drop in the infant mortality rate from three hundred deaths per a thousand births in 1850 to just twenty deaths per a thousand births in 2000.[9] My personal gratitude for such advances increased dramatically in the moments when I watched helplessly as a surgeon wheeled my wife into an operating room with our first child trapped in her birth canal, his body turned upside down and his left ear smashed against his shoulder. As little as fifty years ago, I might have experienced the pain and anguish of losing both a cherished wife and a precious child. Thankfully, however, I was rescued from living that story and taken to a world where on a daily basis I experience the joy, laughter, and beauty of marriage and parenthood.

Certainly, then, I would consider medical technology to be a good and even redemptive thing, and I see this world as better and more advanced than the one of the 1900s. But what do I really mean when I say "more advanced"? What are we advancing toward? Where are we going? One day, both my wife and my children will die, as will I. Would a world with technology that allowed us to live indefinitely—free from disease and even death—be a "better" world than this one?

How we answer these kinds of questions leads us to one of two ways of understanding technology and describing life. In one story, there is a God who is moving humanity along a timeline. He has a purpose and a plan, and there is an end point toward which he is moving all of history. Technology plays a role in this story, but it is a subservient role, not an ultimate one. The only true salvation offered to humanity comes from God himself, through his Son Jesus Christ. Technology offers us foretastes of the lasting healing God will bring, but we still wait for resurrection.

In the other story, there is no God. There is only the advancement of life itself from simple to more complex through chance. This advancement was initially biological in nature, but now the primary means of progressing and advancing life is technological. If there is any salvation or any hope for the future, it will come through the advancement of technology. In biological terms, humanity is known as *Homo sapiens* ("knowing man" or "wise man"), but our true nature is that of *Homo faber* ("making man" or "skilled man") because we advance our kind through the things we make. In this story, the primary problem we face is not sin but the limitations of our carbon-based bodies. Our destiny is to transcend our weak biological bodies in order that we might be born again into eternal machines.

We'll explore these two stories of the world more in chapter 10, but for now we can see that these two versions of life's meaning and direction are at odds. In one story, God is our savior, while in the other, technology is what saves. In one story, God is the source of our resurrection and eternal life; in the other, technology becomes our god who enables our ascension into eternal life. And although the idea that technology can save us has become increasingly popular in the past few centuries, the origin of that story actually began long ago. From the moment Adam and Eve first sinned, and continuing with the life of their son Cain, technology has played a powerful role in the lives and identity of those who reject God. What we see today is the continuation of an unbroken line of humanity that consciously or unconsciously views technology as a god and savior. Today, David Hopper asks, "Has not technology come to embody our chief values—the things we want most out of life?"[10]

But what about us, the people of God? How are we to view technology? Is it an antagonist in the story, a trusty sidekick, or something else? If God is our savior and he wins in the end, does technology even matter? Obviously, we should use technology for good and not for evil, but does anything more need to be said? If it is true that technology has the capacity to shape the world that God made—as well as shape our bodies, minds, and souls—then it seems we should care deeply about our tools. Moreover, if technology plays some role in the story of God redeeming his people, we should care all the more. So let us now turn to the Scriptures and discover where technology began.

QUESTIONS

- What technologies do you appreciate most for the way they help you shape the world into a better place?
- How have certain technologies shaped you in both positive and negative ways, physically and mentally?
- What does your technology mean to you, and what role does it play in what you see as the ultimate meaning and purpose of life?

3

REFLECTION

IF YOU'VE EVER TRIED to learn any computer programming, you might recognize the words "Hello World." That's because whenever a new programming language is created, the first thing its creator does is explain to everyone else how to write a simple program that makes the words "Hello World" appear on-screen. For example, in the widely used programming language C, the code looks something like this:

```
main() {
  printf("hello world");
    }
```

And in PHP, the language used to make early versions of Facebook and the popular website creation tool WordPress, it looks like this:

```
<?php
  echo "Hello World";
    ?>
```

Even if you've never seen the code for a computer program before, these examples should be at least partially readable to you. You can spot the words "Hello World," and you might have guessed that everything else around it tells the computer to send those words to the screen. One of the things that has always fascinated me about programming is that it allows us to create working tools using nothing but words. We don't need any raw materials or physical strength, just pure creativity.

Of course, our task in this book is not to learn about programming but to understand something about what the Scriptures say about technology. And when we open up to the first pages of the Bible, the very first thing we see about God is that he is creative, and that he does a kind of programming of his own. He too is not dependent on raw materials but can instead create by the power of his word. Yet unlike us in our dependence on computers or electricity, God really can create something from nothing.

In this and the coming chapters, we will reexamine familiar biblical stories and look for clues about how we should approach technology. From the outset, I want to make it clear that we won't take the time to acknowledge every nuance or important theological detail in the text. Instead we will simply assume that the Scriptures are true and trustworthy and that they have much to tell us . . . including some things about technology.

God's Creative Process

The first chapter of Genesis portrays God as a creator and maker, someone who brings something wonderous and beautiful out of nothing. But it also does more than that—it also tells us something about *how* he creates. If you carefully observe what God does on each of the six days of creation, you'll notice that there is a repeating pattern, a poetic cadence as God speaks the world into existence. In the first three days, God "separates" and makes spaces, and in the second set of three days he fills those spaces with matching creations. On day one, he creates (or separates) light and darkness, but it's not until day four that he places the sun, moon, and stars in the space God created for them. On day two, he separates the waters above from the waters below, and on day five he fills the sky with birds and the sea with fish.

Then on day three, he creates the dry land, and on day six, he fills it with beasts and with humankind, who we will see have a special purpose.

Day	Form		Content
1	Light and Darkness	4	Sun, Moon, and Stars
2	Sky and Sea	5	Birds and Fish
3	Dry Land	6	Animals and Humans
7	Rest: for Flourishing (Exod. 20) and Freedom (Deut. 5)		

Looking at the creation story this way, we can draw out some important ideas about making. First, we can see that there is an *order and structure* to God's creative process. In the creation myths of other ancient Near East cultures, the gods are in a constant state of chaos and disorder, but here we see Yahweh carefully crafting a rhythmic symphony of life and wonder. This method has a kind of symmetry to it, and symmetry is one of the traditional qualities of aesthetic beauty. In a fallen world, we know there is also beauty in brokenness and restoration, but here we see God in his full glory bringing forth a creation that represents his own majesty and mystery.

In the alignment of days, we can also see that each of God's creations has a *purpose and a proper place*. A bit of programming wisdom commonly attributed to Louis Srygley says, "Without requirements or design, programming is the art of adding bugs to an empty text file." But in the creation story, we can see something like a set of requirements in the first three days when God creates distinct spaces through separations (light/darkness, sky/sea, land/water), and we can see his design in the second three days when he speaks into being creatures appropriate for each space. The stars belong in the darkness of space, just as birds should soar across the sky, and beasts are made to roam the hills. This also means that God's creative process introduces *limits* into the pattern of our world. As we will see in the coming chapters, part of our creative responsibility is to think through what limits we might need to set on our own creative processes and to recognize which messages (content) are appropriate for a given medium (form).

All of this God called "good," but his project was not yet complete. The culmination of his project, the purpose toward which he was working, was the creation of humankind, made in God's image, whom he called "very good." This means that God's creativity is both for his own *glory* and an expression of divine *love*. God is not creating structure for its own sake but as a reflection of the triune life of God. Perhaps this is why the creation account is not in the form of detailed instruction but of poetry. As Makoto Fujimura writes, "I like to think, and many Hebrew scholars attest, that God the Creator sang the creation into being."[1]

Finally, we also see that God has built into his creative rhythm a *pattern of rest*. We humans need rest because we are limited and get tired, but a limitless God does not tire. This means that he instituted the pattern of rest for a different reason, and the Pentateuch actually gives us two. In Exodus 20, the Israelites are told to keep the Sabbath pattern as a celebration of the flourishing of creation. If we never rest (perhaps with some screen-free time), we are never able to appreciate the work we have done and declare it "good." Then, in Deuteronomy 5, God connects the idea of rest to the Israelites' slavery in Egypt, meaning that rest is an expression of freedom. Today we have an amazing array of time-saving devices, and yet when we never rest from them, we need to ask if they are truly our liberators or if we have allowed them to keep us enslaved. What we see in God's creative process is a combination of beauty, order, rhythm, purpose, love, and limits, all of which should inform our own creativity and use of technology.

How We're Programmed

Zooming deeper into God's creative process, we notice that he gives each of his creations a specific purpose and function. To the stars he gives the job of separating day and night and marking out the seasons. To the plants he gives the job of sprouting fruit and seed. To the fish—which the Hebrew literally calls "the swimming things"—God says simply, "Swim." And to the birds—literally "the flying things"—he says, "Fly." What they are made to *do*—shining, sprouting, swimming, and flying—in part defines what they *are*.

What, then, are human beings? If all the other creatures are defined by what they do, what is the thing that we humans do that makes us human? In other words, how did God program us?

Later on the sixth day, God answered this question by defining humanity not as creatures that sprout, swim, or fly but by saying, "Let us make humankind in our image" (Gen. 1:26 NET). This means that our job, and the essence of what it is to be human, is to reflect God's image to the rest of creation, and this gives every man, woman, and child unmatched dignity and value. Of course, many theologians have worn out their keyboards trying to demystify what it means to reflect God's image, but we can explore what it means using four categories.

First, humans display God's ability to think rationally. Although some animals display a form of intelligence, humans are clearly distinct from the rest of the created order. Second, many thinkers have noticed the plural language referring to God ("let *us*") and proposed that humans reflect God's relationality. In our sin we attempt to live independent of our need for God and others, but God originally designed humans to function in a deeply interdependent way that reflects the tri-personhood of God. Third, just as God is the ruler over the entire universe and all created things, his image bearers are to rule over this tiny little planet. In Genesis 1 God commanded humanity to "have dominion" and "subdue" the earth (v. 28 KJV).

These three facets of humanity—our rational thinking, our relational nature, and our call to subdue the earth—are all undoubtedly reflections of God's nature. But we discover a final category as we move into Genesis 2, and it is this one that needs a bit more explanation.

Whereas Genesis 1 offers a panoramic view of the entire universe, Genesis 2 zooms in on God's design and production of humanity. Unlike the lush, full world of Genesis 1, chapter 2 begins with a barren, lifeless landscape where "no plant had yet sprung up" (v. 5). Part of the reason for this was that "God had not sent rain," but the other issue was that "there was no one to work the ground." In Hebrew, there's a little wordplay going on because the word for "ground" (*adama*) sounds like the word for human (*adam*). Literally it reads, "There was no *adam* for the *adama*." Then God responds by picking up some of the dust from the dry, barren landscape and sculpting that dust into the first human being.

But God's image bearer wasn't meant to live in an arid wasteland, and so before God does anything with Adam, he first plants the garden of Eden and fills it with tall trees, ripe fruit, and flowing rivers. Once the garden is prepared, God gently sets Adam down within and gives him a simple job: "cultivate it and keep it" (Gen. 2:15 NASB1995). The air has flying things that fly, the sea has swimming things that swim, and now, finally, the *adama* has *Adam* to cultivate and keep it.

This tells us something important about both human nature and the garden. It means that God designed the garden—even before the fall, sin, and death—in such a way that it needed to be worked on. It's not that there was anything wrong with the garden; it's just that God didn't intend for it to stay the way that it was. Instead, God wanted Adam to "cultivate" or "till" or "work" what he found in the garden and make something new out of it. In the verses that follow, Genesis names four rivers, which might seem out of place in the story. But notice that it says, "The gold of that land is good; aromatic resin and onyx are also there" (Gen. 2:12). This is indicating that God created the garden not as an end point but as a starting place. Adam's job was to take the raw materials of the earth—from the wood of the trees, to the rocks on the ground, to the metal buried deep within the earth—and create new things from them. In a sense, Adam was to take the "natural" world—what God made—and fashion it into something else—something not entirely "natural" but sanctioned by God. If the fish were programmed to swim and the birds were programmed to fly, then humans were programmed to make things from what God has made. God declared his creation of the world "good" and his image bearers "very good," and this means that their creations are also "good."

And just as God created structures and limits as part of his own creative process, he also sets some boundaries for Adam. As we all know, God warned Adam not to eat from the Tree of the Knowledge of Good and Evil. But God also put limits on the way Adam was to create. The command to "cultivate the garden" was coupled with the command to "keep the garden." That word *keep* can also mean "guard" or "watch over," and it conveys the idea that Adam was not only to shape the garden but also to maintain something of its original form. He was not to over-cultivate it or use its raw materials in a way that would unnecessarily harm it or God's creatures. Similarly, to "have dominion" does not mean to dominate, misuse, or destroy. Although some Christians have allowed discussions of the environment to become politicized, we find in Genesis 2 a theology of creation care wherein God sets limits on what we should do with his creation. God seems to be asking us to strike a careful balance between natural and unnatural, between the acts of cultivating and keeping.

Within these limits, Adam could do whatever he wanted in the garden, rearranging and creating from it as he saw fit. He could add a row of stones around trees he liked or make a bridge over one of the rivers. He could build a storage shed out of shells or collect seeds and plant them in rows. Whatever he chose to do, he would be taking what God had made and remaking it into a creation of his own. And in doing so, Adam would be reflecting the creativity of his Creator (who, at this point in the story, has done little but create). As a father, I delighted in dumping a box of Lego bricks on the floor and seeing what my children would create with them, and God too delights in seeing what we will create with what he has given us. This is one of the reasons why I resist calling creativity and technology neutral. Instead, when God creates, he calls it "good," and I think our ability to create is also "good." And yet, as we will see, the things we make are also complex in their meaning and significance.

Creativity Is Image-Bearing and Meaning-Making

The final aspect of our role as God's image bearers, then, is our ability to create. When we cultivate the garden—when we make things from what God has made—we are reflecting the image of God.

But something else important happens when we create. By choosing to put rocks around one set of trees and not another, Adam and Eve would be making a decision about what was important to them. By adding a bridge over this part of that river, they would be making a choice about the way they thought things should work. With each creative act, they would be prioritizing one set of choices over another, determining what mattered to them, and what content was appropriate for which container. As they modeled these behaviors to their children—and their children in turn modeled those same behaviors to the next generation—the first couple's choices would form the basis of what humanity considered important and meaningful.

This idea that the things we make have meaning brings us to the concept of "culture" which is related to the word *cultivate* that we have been discussing. Now, there are probably as many definitions and views of culture as there were trees in the garden—and the word *culture* brings with it things like "culture wars," "high culture" versus "low culture," and the debate over "Christ and culture." To simplify this, we can use Ken Myers's definition of culture, which is "what we make of the world."[2] This definition has a double meaning in that culture is both the physical things we make from the world as well as the meaning we derive from those things.

Theologian Stanley Grenz groups what we create into four broad categories: things, images, rituals, and language.[3] A *thing* is simply any physical object that people create, from a bridge over a river to the utensils with which we eat. *Images*, though objects also, are designed to represent something else, like a company logo, a symbol on a traffic sign, or the cross that represents our faith. *Rituals* are what we do with those things and images, including the time of year when we plant vegetables, how we wake up in the morning, how we brush our teeth, and the way we make coffee. Finally, *language* is the tool we use to share the meaning of these objects, images, and rituals. To these four categories, we might also add *places* to include the way we use parks, roads, buildings, and other structures to turn an empty space into a place of meaning.

As we create and use things, images, rituals, language, and places with others, we are sharing not only those items but also what they mean to us. The word we use to summarize this transfer of meaning is *culture*. In fact, these passages in Genesis 1 and 2 have sometimes been called the "cultural mandate" because theologians find in them the command and responsibility for humans to create culture. We all exist within multiple overlapping cultures, which can include the region of the country we live in, our race or ethnicity, our religious subgroup, and even our families and workplaces. Each of these intersecting cultures shape who we are and what we value. My dear friend and pastor Barry Jones adds to this by saying that the elements of culture—things, images, rituals, language, and places—mediate three things to us: identity, meaning, and values. Theologian Emil Brunner captured this idea when he wrote that culture is the "materialization of meaning,"[4] but I did not fully understand what he meant until I experienced it firsthand.

An Altar in the Garden

A few years after I graduated from college, I started to wonder how my mom managed to raise four great kids as a single parent. One day she answered my question by taking me on a walk at a nearby park we used to visit when I was growing up. As we were walking along the path, my mom stopped for a moment to point out a small pile of rocks a few yards off into the woods.

The pile was small enough that I hadn't noticed it, but once she pointed to it, I could see that it was human-made. The rocks obviously couldn't have gotten that way themselves—someone had collected and arranged them. After looking at them for a minute, I asked her, "What is it?"

My mom started to talk about how hard it was on her when my dad left. He gave her a lot of financial support and came to see us regularly, but she still felt crushed by the weight of raising us alone. Most of the time, the only thing she felt strong enough to do was pray for us. So every day while we were off at school, she would walk out to this spot and spend a few hours begging God to protect us. As God answered her prayers, she found some nearby rocks and built this little altar to mark the place where God had been faithful to our family.

As she told her story, that ordinary pile of rocks transformed into something of enormous meaning to me. My mother had made this little place more important than the places in front of us and the places behind us. God had done something meaningful for my family, and my mother materialized that meaning into a tangible, visible form. She did this by taking what

God had made—a few simple rocks—and remaking it into something that reflected the creativity and goodness of God.

Growing up, my mom never talked about her little altar, but when she finally told me about it, it changed me. I could never again see myself as a person whom God had forgotten. My identity was altered such that I now see myself as a person who was an answer to prayer. Those stones said I would not be who I was if God had not acted.

Using Grenz's terminology, my mom's altar was a *thing* around which she had built a *ritual* of consistently praying for her children, turning a space into a *place*. When my mother shared her altar with me—expressing the significance of the stone through *language*—it was deeply meaningful to me, and it mediated the value of a life of prayerfulness as well as a new sense of identity.

While the example of my mom's altar might seem extraordinary, this mediation of values happens anytime we create—and even when we rearrange—everyday things. For example, imagine that you walked into a room full of twenty chairs. If those chairs were arranged in four rows of five with a podium up front, you would immediately know this was some kind of classroom with a clear authority figure. But if those same chairs were arranged in a circle, you would tend to interpret it as a group-oriented setting where everyone is equal. The "culture" of the room would be determined by both the presence of chairs and the arrangement of them. Every day, we participate in dozens of these little cultures. Our homes, offices, churches, cities, and countries each encompass a unique set of things, images, rituals, language, and places that forms its identity and communicates meaning and value. Some of the cultural systems we participate in promote the values of the kingdom of God, but others can be dehumanizing, so we need to learn to see these systems at work in order to learn how to redirect them toward human flourishing.

This discussion of culture making may sound great in an ideal world free from sin, but you might also be thinking that we don't live in the garden of Eden. The wickedness and suffering we see today has led some to believe that culture is synonymous with worldliness. This makes it hard to believe that culture and technology actually existed in the garden. Yet the word translated as "cultivate" in Genesis 2 is elsewhere translated "till," an action that assumes the use of tools. This seems to indicate that using tools was a part of God's design for humanity even before the fall. But even more importantly, if we look carefully at Genesis 2, we'll see that the first elements of culture—and the first tools that both shaped the world and the humans who used them—were created *in the garden.*

The First Technology

If you ask a cultural anthropologist or evolutionary biologist to identify the most important tool developed by early humans, they will invariably say it was language. Even monkeys use stone tools, but it was language that allowed humans to build and share knowledge. Interestingly, Genesis seems to agree with this line of thinking.

After God put Adam in the garden to "cultivate and keep it," he gave Adam his first creative task. As God created the animals, he "brought them to the man to see what he would name them; and whatever the man called each living creature, that was its name" (Gen. 2:19). Genesis goes on to say, "the man gave names to all the livestock, the birds in the sky and all the wild animals" (v. 20).

The traditional reading of this story emphasizes that this exercise was designed to show Adam that none of the animals could serve as a "suitable helper" for him (remember that word *helper*). But the text also indicates that God had a second purpose in mind: he wanted "to see what [Adam] would name them" (v. 19). In other words, he wanted to watch as Adam *created* language.

There in the garden, as he created words and names that didn't exist before, Adam started reflecting the image of God. These words would serve as the lens through which Eve and their children would see those creatures. Now, we don't ordinarily think of language as a technology, but language is one of our most ancient and powerful tools. This is because language does not merely communicate information. It also helps us categorize and understand the world, embed our values in conversation, know we are part of a group with a shared identity, and, as we'll find below, we can even use language to *do* things.

When my son was learning his first words, my wife and I loved to see how his little mind organized the world around the words he knew. The first animal name he learned was "duck," and since that was the only word he knew, he called everything "duck" . . . dogs, cats, birds, elephants, and every other living creature. He was constantly pointing to anything that moved and shouting, "Duck!" Thankfully, he soon started learning additional categories like fish and cat and bird, and the more words he learned, the more he could communicate with us. Later he began learning his colors, and I loved watching his little face as he studied an object, categorized it, and then blurted out a new word. Where he used to just see a collection of undifferentiated objects, he could now organize that visual space using the colors and names we had given him.

Beyond categorization, sometimes the names we give animals emphasize one of their characteristics over another. For example, when we think of a blue jay, we see it primarily in terms of its color, but a woodpecker is named not for how it looks but for what it does. In this way, words often have a series of assumptions and values built into them. For example, the word *bachelor* describes a man whom our culture defines as old enough to have married but who has not done so. The existence of the word *bachelor* shows that English-speaking cultures value men marrying at a certain age. Similarly, the words *homemaker* and *stay-at-home mom* convey different expectations about the roles women are often expected to take. Earlier we came across the word *helper* in Genesis, which in English can convey the sense of someone secondary. But in Hebrew, the word *ezer* is often used to describe God coming to the aid of his people (Exod. 18:4; Pss. 70:5; 124:8; Hos. 13:9), which means that word is intended to convey the full equality of male and female.

Let's consider the built-in meaning of some other words. As you're reading this, take a moment to visualize two people—a doctor and a nurse. Picture what they are wearing, where they are standing, their height, age, and so on. If I asked an artificial intelligence (AI) to do the same task, to generate an image of a doctor and a nurse from some training data, it's very likely that you and the AI would both picture a male doctor and a female nurse. That's because even though both women and men are fully capable of doing either job, English-speaking cultures have embedded into the language the (incorrect) idea the doctors should be men and nurses should be women. This assumption runs so deep that when programmers use machine learning to teach an AI how to understand English, the AI picks up on the bias built into our language and learns to make the same correlation.[5] Similar to raising children, we have to teach our AI to unlearn some of the biases built into our language if we want our machines to understand the world through the values we say we possess.

This example is meant to show that language operates as a kind of medium between us and the world, a tool that shapes what we see and don't see. As Adam gave names to the animals, perhaps emphasizing one trait over another, so too our words shape how and what we see in the world. For example, the Bible was written in Hebrew and Greek, and both of these languages have a different word for "you" when referring to one person (singular) and "you" when referring to a group of people (plural). In modern English, we tend to use "you" for both singular and plural, but there are regionally specific plural words like "y'all" (Southern US) or "you lot" (UK). If we used one of these plural terms to translate a popular verse like Jeremiah 29:11, we might see something different in the verse: "'For I know the plans I have for *y'all*,' declares the LORD, 'plans to prosper *y'all* and not to harm *y'all*, plans to give *y'all* hope and a future'" (based on NIV, see more at yallversion.com).

Language, along with various accents and derivatives, can also be used to form boundaries around groups of people. Judges 12:4–6, tells the story of when the Israelite tribe of Ephraim tried to sneak across the river from their enemies the Gileadites. The Gileadites tested them by asking them to say the word "Shibboleth." Anyone who couldn't make the "sh" sound pronounced it as "Sibboleth" and was killed!

Today, accents and word usage still function to determine who is in and who is out in a group. The same kind of linguistic boundaries sometimes occur in modern technological communication. For example, different generations and cultures use acronyms, emoticons, and even punctuation quite differently. If you receive a text from someone significantly older or younger than you, it might literally feel like a different language or a new, distinct culture. Those who use the words and symbols with the right "accent" are in, while those who don't are out. This fits with the idea that culture mediates not only values and meaning but also identity.

Language also goes beyond categorization, values, and group identity—it can function in a tool-like manner when we use it to *accomplish* something. For example, the words "I now pronounce you man and wife" perform the function of marrying a couple. And the words "I nominate Rebecca as team captain" have actually *done* something. When one person says to another, "I hate you," we say, "Those were hurtful words," because the words didn't just transfer the state of hatred—they actually functioned to wound the hearer. Linguists use the term "speech acts" to describe this aspect of language,[6] and they have identified dozens of things we *do* with language: we confess, forgive, frighten, inspire, and so on.

Embracing Our Reflective Role

It turns out that what I thought was special about programming—creating things with words—is not so unique after all. From the opening pages of Genesis, we find God speaking the entire universe into existence and Adam making up words as some of his first creative acts. We have seen that language is our first tool and an example of how humans create within the creation of God, imbuing each creation with value and meaning. God designed the world in such a way that it was meant to be cultivated and shaped by humanity, and when we create, we are operating as God's image bearers. This means that our creative power, including technology, is a God-given good.

But as God has shown us with his own creative process, when we create and use technology, we have a call and responsibility to do it within the boundaries of order, beauty, and human dignity. As Mary McCleary has written, "Good craftsmanship reflects the maker's respect for himself, the materials of creation, as well as a high regard for the user or viewer."[7] God delights in our good creations while also urging us to treat all of his creation with care and respect.

QUESTIONS

- What creative skills has God given you that you can use to reflect his image and fulfill our call to make from what he has made?
- What cultures are you a part of, and what are the things, images, rituals, language, and places that are significant to those cultures?
- How can you use language in a way that creates, builds up, and accomplishes rather than separates or perpetuates biases?

4

DEFINITION

AT A HOUSEWARMING PARTY for a friend, I met the CEO of an up-and-coming technology company who also happened to be a passionate Christian man. Since our interests overlapped, we started a lively discussion about technology and culture.

As we were talking about the direction technology will take us in the coming years, he stopped abruptly and said, "Wait a minute. That would mean we'd have to consider just about *everything* to be technology—cars, boats, phones, air-conditioning, and on and on." In that moment, we both realized that we'd been using the word *technology* with slightly different meanings. For him, technology meant electronic gadgets like phones, robotic vacuum cleaners, and things built on blockchain, but it didn't include mechanically oriented things like cars, espresso machines, and microwaves. Yet he also said things like, "My company offers more advanced technological solutions than any of our competitors." In that case, he wasn't using "technology" to refer to physical gadgets but more broadly to the kind of "high-tech knowledge" that businesses use to solve problems.

So what is "technology" exactly? Does it refer only to electronics, or does it include mechanical devices as well? Can it also mean a special kind of working knowledge? We learned in the previous chapter that creating and using tools is a good, image-bearing activity, but today's technology seems far removed from the biblical command to cultivate and keep the garden and from the kinds of tools used by biblical characters like Moses and Isaiah. Is there any relationship between the technology of the Scriptures and technology today?

The following pages will equip you for thrilling dinner conversations by narrowing down where technology fits into the commands to cultivate the earth and serve as God's image bearers. First, by briefly tracing the historical usage of the word *technology*, we'll look at how we arrived at such confusion over its meaning. Next we'll attempt to compare ancient tools of the biblical world to today's enormously complex technology by dissecting technology into four components. And finally, I'll propose a simple definition of technology that we can use in the rest of the book.

Origins of "Technology"

The English term *technology* is composed of two Greek words: *téchnē*, which means "craft, skill, or art," and *logía*, which refers to the systematic study of a subject. But unlike the way we have been discussing technology, the Greek term *téchnē* referred to a person's skill in making things, not the tools they used to do so.

When we say someone is "into technology," we usually mean they own a lot of new devices and enjoy using them, but when the Greeks called someone a *tektōn* (in chapter 9, we'll find that this was the term used to describe the occupation of Jesus's father, Joseph), it meant that the person had spent a great deal of time learning and honing a particular craft. That craft could be working with wood, stone, metal, or some other physical material. Since there were no factories to mass-produce things, every painting, every knife, every sculpture, and every horseshoe was a unique work that reflected the maker's *téchnē*.

Téchnē could even refer to writing poetry or drafting plans. In fact, the only ancient writer to combine the words *téchnē* and *logía* into our term *technologia* was the philosopher Aristotle, who used the word to describe the systematic study of grammar, speech, and writing. The Greeks and the ancient world in general did not distinguish between art and technology as we do today but grouped them together with a wider range of skills and knowledge. Plato and Aristotle didn't have a particularly high view of *téchnē*, and despite the fact that both Jesus and Paul worked with the technological tools of their trades, early Christians tended to treat making merely as something that had to be done. For example, Augustine's *The City of God* contrasts spiritual virtue with human making, appearing first to praise it— "There have been discovered and perfected, by the natural genius of man, innumerable arts and skills which minister not only to the necessities of life but also to human enjoyment"—but then ultimately concluding that "all these favors taken together are but the fragmentary solace allowed us in a life condemned to misery."[1] Hugh of St. Victor (1096–1141) was one of the first Christian thinkers to value what he called "mechanical philosophy," which included technology, carpentry, agriculture, and medicine, alongside theoretical philosophy (theology, mathematics, and physics) and practical philosophy (ethics, economics, and politics).

It wasn't until much later, during the 1600s, that the term *technology* found its way into the English language. At that time, people used it in much the same way the Greeks did, referring to any skill or craft that a person might learn. But the 1600s was also a turning point in history with its explosion in scientific knowledge, and inventors started experimenting with the first large-scale machinery. Up to this point, most human tools were small enough for a single individual to use, but the newer, larger machines needed wind, water, or animals to power them. The new machines also gave humanity unprecedented new powers to manipulate and process the materials of the earth, and this led scientists like Galileo and philosophers like Descartes to begin speaking in terms of "crafting" the world and "shaping" it according to the needs of humanity.

For the first time, humans saw their abilities extend beyond cultivating their little plots of land to actually dominating the natural world. Over time, as these machines grew larger and more powerful, people started distinguishing between "fine arts," like painting and sculpting, and the "mechanical arts" (i.e., machine making). Eventually, they stopped using the word *technology* to refer to crafting skills and began using it exclusively in reference to mechanical arts.

Previously the skill of mechanical arts had been passed down from experienced masters to the next generation through a process of apprenticeship. But during the Industrial Revolution of the 1700s and 1800s, large factories began to pop up all over Europe. These factories could produce thousands of identical goods much faster than individuals could produce unique works. As blacksmiths, weavers, and others shuttered their doors, apprenticeship as a means of teaching was also pushed aside in favor of a more formal setting for distributing skills. Factories needed workers who had the same knowledge and skill sets so that they could be easily interchanged; therefore, education needed to be standardized.

This led to people using the word *technology* to refer to studying the mechanical arts in a formal educational setting. Up to this point, technology meant *practicing* the mechanical arts (i.e., making things), but in this period it came to mean the *study of* the mechanical arts. Harvard professor Jacob Bigelow is credited with being the first to use technology this way in his textbook *Elements of Technology*, published in 1829. A few decades later, in 1861, the Massachusetts Institute of Technology was founded with this educational meaning of technology embedded in its name.

At the end of the 1800s, technology still meant either practicing or studying mechanical arts, but no one was using it to refer to tools as we do today. This all changed in the early 1900s when people started using the word *technology* both for the *tools* used in mechanical arts (such as wrenches and welders) as well as the *things* made by mechanical arts (chairs, cars, boats, and so on). If you're keeping track, this means that "technology" now has at least four different meanings: (1) the *skill* of making things, (2) the *study* of the skill of making things, (3) the *tools* used to make things, and (4) the *things* made with these tools.

Part of this confusion arose because many European languages had multiple, distinct terms for these aspects of the single English word *technology*.

For example, German and French use the word *technologie* to refer to the study of making industrial products, but they have different words (*arts et métiers* in French and *Technik* in German) to refer to the act of making those industrial products.

Exponential Growth

Another reason *technology* came to refer to so many things is that the complexity of our tools began to increase exponentially. Historians say that from the dawn of human history until around 1650, the rate of technological change was relatively flat. New inventions—aqueducts, gunpowder, or the printing press—would come along every few hundred years, but 1650 kicked off three distinct ages of tremendous increase in technological innovation: the period from 1650 to 1850, from 1850 to 1950, and from 1950 to 2000.

Long before 1650, when someone invented a new tool, it was used only in the same general region where it was invented, as there was not transportation or communication in place to quickly share it with the rest of the world. But in the period of time leading up to 1650, the world's transportation and communication infrastructure progressed in leaps and bounds. Printed books allowed people to share scientific knowledge and technological skill much faster than before, and that knowledge could be quickly transported around the world using newer, more reliable ships. Each new invention and discovery expanded on the previous ones, leading to a more rapid pace of development. To top it off, the population of the world doubled from 1650 to 1850. Sadly, much of this growth and expansion came on the backs of slaves, and those who traveled around the world with new inventions tended to see themselves as superior to those they encountered, leading to a complex and toxic mix of technology, ethnicity, and religion that still impacts our cultures today.

In the century from 1850 to 1950, the population of the earth doubled again, and there was another rapid increase in technological development, laying the foundation for many of the tools we use today. While the period from 1650 to 1850 was primarily focused on building larger and more powerful machines far stronger than human and animal power could offer, the developments from 1850 to 1950 were focused on replicating human senses. Whereas the machine age produced mechanical arms and legs, the next hundred years produced electronic eyes, ears, and brains.

The electronic eye came in the form of the photograph (which was initially purely mechanical). Though attempts at photography had gone on for centuries, the technology was finally perfected in this era. Those first cameras paved the way for every iteration of visual technology we have today, from the earliest televisions to today's augmented and virtual reality experiences. Electronic ears and mouths came in the form of Edison's phonograph, the first device to capture and play back sounds. Before that time, music could only be experienced in a live setting, and verbal communication could only take place face-to-face. The first electronic brains also found their origin in this period with the invention of the telegraph. For the first time, information could be transported instantaneously from any place in the world to another. Knowledge was no longer confined to the speed of a horse or a ship but could be shared in an instant.

Then, during the next fifty years from 1950 to 2000, the world's population again doubled, and the invention of the microchip accelerated all the prior inventions to warp speed. Since the 2000s, all of the technology invented in the era from 1850 to 2000—radios, TVs, phones, computers, the internet, and so on—has been condensed into the glowing rectangles nearly all of us carry in our pockets, and our phones are in turn powered by the mechanical processes pioneered from 1650 to 1850.

This means that for the past few centuries, both the human population and the complexity and power of technology have been growing exponentially. Our network of technology and resources is so vast today that it's almost unrecognizably different from anything prior to the 1650s. It's even harder to see how today's technology relates to what God said to Adam in the garden. But if we break our technology down into more manageable parts, we'll see that it is still very much related to God's charge to cultivate and keep the earth.

Four Layers of Technology

To help comprehend the enormous complexity of technology today, philosopher Stephen J. Kline subdivides technology into four discernible layers, each of which builds on the others.[2] We will use his laycring as a guide for comparing ancient and modern technology, and then use it to create a definition of technology that encompasses both.

Technology as hardware. Kline writes that at the most basic level, "technology" is the physical pieces of hardware that we use, including phones, clocks, shovels, belts, thermometers, guns, and cans of root beer. For Kline, any physical object that does not occur naturally in our world counts as technological hardware. Kline does not take the time to define "natural" and "unnatural," but his words nicely fit the distinction that we found back in Genesis between what God has made and what we make out of God's creation.

If you take a moment to look around you, you'll probably find a combination of both "natural" things like people, pets, and plants, as well as "unnatural" things like chairs, beds, desks, lights, water fountains, and so on. According to Kline's definition, all of these human-made goods would be considered technology, making them similar to Grenz's category of "things" among the cultural goods humans create. This is a good starting point, but notice that it lumps tools together with art and everything else people make. This means that we'll need to define technology in such a way that we can distinguish it from other things people make.

Technology as manufacturing. Taking a step back from the devices in our pockets and on our desks, Kline's second layer makes a distinction between those pieces of hardware and the tools and systems used to make the hardware, such as factories and assembly lines. "Technology as manufacturing" includes the vat holding the molten steel for our cars, the robots that put together our phones, and even the complex sociotechnical systems that need to be in place for the factories to operate. This includes everything from the people running the machines to the electrical grid powering the plant to the legislation that regulates the industry.

This layer of technology is significant because it was largely nonexistent before the Industrial Revolution. Most of the tools before that era could be used on their own without support from a large, complex network. Once a knife or a shovel was made, it was useful by itself. But most of the tools we use today like computers and phones are useless without batteries, power outlets, cell towers, the internet, and so on. Similarly, building a modern automobile takes entire systems of metal purification, computer programming, and oil and gas production.

Another difference between today's technology and the technology of the past is that the tools used before the 1800s involved mostly the basic materials that Adam could have found lying around the garden of Eden. This meant that one person could design, build, and use a tool. In contrast, modern technology uses a variety of exotic materials that the average person knows little about. It now takes an army of designers, manufacturers, transporters, and retailers to create and distribute a piece of modern technology. As our tools grow more and more complex, the network of people and machines needed to make them grows as well, sometimes spanning multiple continents.

Our understanding of technology, then, needs to encompass both the kinds of hardware used in earlier eras as well as the more complex, interconnected systems that make our life possible today. It also forces us to acknowledge that the tools we use today don't exist in isolation but are deeply integrated with the lives of those around us. Unlike a shovel that is largely inert and disconnected, our phones are constantly connected to large companies who profit from our use of them, which means we must also be aware of how we can be manipulated in our behavior or beliefs. In other words, there is no one inside our shovels trying to get us to dig more holes, but there are people on the other side of our phones who profit each time we pick them up!

This aspect of technology has also become increasingly important as people buy more products online and have them shipped, sometimes on the same day. To make this possible, companies like Amazon maintain vast networks of distribution centers and work to continuously improve the algorithms and processes that get all your items into a brown box of just the right size. We could expand Kline's category to "technology as distribution" or "technology as network" to account for this largely hidden layer of technology, which includes the cloud servers that back up our files and photos and the data-tracking systems companies use to monitor our behaviors.

Technology as methodology. Kline's third layer of technology is the knowledge and know-how necessary for making technological products. This usage of technology refers neither to the physical products nor to the machines used to make the products but to the routines, methods, and skills used in the process of making modern hardware, writing modern software, and doing modern business.

Most companies and churches have quite a bit of technology as hardware, but they also need an "IT guy" (there's that language bias again—let's say "IT person" instead) who has the specialized knowledge of how it all works. At a higher level, consulting firms make billions of dollars refining and streamlining the methods (or "business processes") that companies use to make their hardware. When the company IBM was first created, its name described what it made—international business machines. But the company later found that building machines was no longer profitable. In response, IBM transformed itself into a "technology firm," advertising specialized knowledge that can make businesses run more efficiently. (My CEO friend at the dinner party was referring to this layer of technology when he talked about what his business could offer others.)

This layer of technology is often the most overlooked, but like all rituals we create, it too has the capacity to influence the way we see the world. Theologian Jacques Ellul worried that technology as methodology often shapes our emotional, spiritual, and relational worlds in ways that aren't always compatible with our Christian faith. He wrote that in the modern world we have become so accustomed to thinking in a technological way (what he called *La Technique*) that we apply technological values to almost every problem without even realizing it. For example, Neil Postman wrote that it was not until 1792 that the first numerical grade was given in a school setting.[3] That year, William Farish, a tutor at the University of Cambridge, tried to come up with a uniform way of evaluating students that was as consistent as what a machine would produce. Instead of tracking the progress of each student individually and holistically, Farish applied technological ideas to education and, as a result, created the numerical ranking of student progress that we still use today. It now seems impossible to even conceive of modern education without grades. According to Ellul and Postman, the more we use technology, the more it mediates to us the value of addressing problems with technological solutions. When we encounter a challenge or hindrance, we immediately search for a technological method or tool that can overcome it, further reinforcing technology's importance in our lives.

We even apply this kind of machinelike thinking to problems that arise in the church. For example, when we apply *La Technique* to the Great Commission to "make disciples," the result is often the creation of a "discipleship program." Churches urge their members to go through the program in hope that they will all come through the process as uniformly mature Christians. Of course, it's wonderful when everyone in our church gets the chance to be theologically and biblically educated, but we can easily err into treating the spiritual growth of a human soul as if it were a simple mechanical process. Then, when we purchase "proven tools for spiritual growth" that don't seem to "work," we assume that we need to find and purchase a different tool, never considering that such a thing might not exist. We see this even more explicitly in religious apps that use features of gamification to encourage reading, prayer, or other quantifiable activities. Similarly, when we shift discipleship, education, and church into digital forms, we have to ask how the methodology of the technology might influence what we are doing.

I don't mean to be critical of biblical education or online expressions of faith. (After all, I do both for a living!) I merely mean to point out that technology as methodology operates powerfully beneath the surface, often encouraging us to apply the values and priorities of machines to our endeavors. When we think about defining technology, we need to remember that it's not just the physical goods that are important but also the way they teach us to think, behave, and solve problems. We also need to be aware that the people who have this knowledge or skill often have disproportionate power and authority, both in business and even within the church.

Technology as social usage. Kline's final layer of technology is at the opposite end of the spectrum from *La Technique*. If technology as methodology is the knowledge of how to create hardware, technology as social usage is the customs and rules (or rituals) around how we *use* the hardware. For example, our society has created a host of conventions around how we should and shouldn't use cars. We have turn signals, speed limits, yielding rules, and dozens of other conventions designed to keep us safe. Before we are granted a license to drive, we have to demonstrate not only that we can operate a car but that we can do so within these socially defined rules. With social media, there are constantly shifting norms of how to appropriately use each new platform (but notice that there is no license required!).

Most of the tools invented before the machine age did not require complex rules because those tools generally could not do much harm other than to the person using them. But as technology grows more complex, it gains the ability to affect more people, and that requires increasingly complex social conventions to use technology in harmonious ways.

Here at the social level we begin to observe some interesting things about the way technology and culture interact. Sometimes a new technology will create an entirely new way of experiencing an older cultural practice. For example, we mentioned that before Edison invented a way to record and play back sound, music was only experienced with live performers. The advent of recorded music eliminated the need for performers to be present and created new social conventions like gathering around the radio to listen to recorded music. Then in 1979, Sony released the first Walkman. Its batteries made music portable, and its headphones meant that for the first time music was primarily experienced by the individual rather than the group. This experience morphed several times with mixtapes, burnable discs, digital music, and streaming platforms, each of which made the powerful emotional experience of music tailored specifically to the listener.

The result was a role reversal of artist and listener. Instead of the artist controlling the flow of the music, now listeners used playlists to control the order of the artists. People now walk down the street experiencing a world that no one else can see or hear. It also changed the relationship between members of the audience. Before recorded music and headphones, people had to listen to music together. And before digital music, people often heard a song for the first time when a friend shared a physical medium, but now we often encounter a new artist through a recommendation made by an algorithm. This creates a culture known only to the individual listener, separated from all other communities.

These examples show us that changes in technology result in changes in culture. These changes are not entirely predictable, however, because the social usage pattern of a technology is often different from the intent of its designers. For example, Twitter was originally designed largely as an interface for sending text messages to a large group of friends. One person would send a message to Twitter, and Twitter would then disseminate it as a text message to mobile phones subscribed to that specific person. In essence, Twitter was initially designed as a one-way broadcast mechanism.

However, Twitter users began using the service in ways its designers did not entirely foresee. They began using it less and less through text messages and more and more online through the main Twitter website and third-party programs. And instead of always broadcasting one-way messages, they began using it for two-way conversations. To make these conversations work, users created their own conventions for how to reply to one another and share messages across groups of friends. Eventually Twitter adopted the @reply standard, as well as a version of the retweet, but they did so long after these other uses had become social conventions.

The examples of the evolution of usage in music and social media show us that just as tools both shape the world and their users, technology can also shape entire cultures, and in turn be shaped by those cultures. Individuals within cultures create tools, then others within the culture begin using a given tool, creating social conventions around its usage. Those conventions then become incorporated into the culture itself, and over time the tools and conventions around the tools begin to shape the thinking of the individuals who use them. This pattern has been called the "social shaping of technology," and we will explore it more in chapter 6.

Technology Defined

Kline's four layers help us dissect the complexity of modern technology and see how it has become intertwined with almost everything we do. In chapter 11, we'll devote space to considering some important differences between ancient tools and modern devices, but Kline's four layers also help us see how the word "technology" can encompass both. We are therefore able to create a simple, encompassing definition of technology. The following definition is my own, derived from and indebted to the work of Stephen Monsma: technology is the human activity of using tools to transform God's creation for practical purposes.[4] At just thirteen words, it may not seem like much, so let's unpack it a bit.

First, because technology is more than just the tools we use, we define technology as an *activity* that we do and that we are constantly doing. But we don't do this activity as individuals in isolation. Rather, technology takes place within the context of *human* communities, and when we use technology we must recognize that our use of it affects those around us. Of course, technology involves *using tools*. Here I am using "tool" in a very broad sense to include physical *tools* like wrenches and airplanes, as well as modern *devices* like phones and VR headsets, and even the *methods* we use to manage them. What makes a tool distinct from other cultural goods is that it is used to *transform God's creation*. The aesthetic qualities of a work of art may transform our hearts and minds through an encounter with beauty, but tools have a more transactional function: transforming the natural world. We might say that we *hold* tools, but we *behold* art. We must also remember that even as we use tools to transform God's creation, we, the tool users, are also part of that transformation.

When we use tools for transformation, we do so for some *practical end*.

This is meant to acknowledge that what we are transforming is God's, but also that humans do so for their own purposes. Sometimes those ends are in line with what God would want—balancing the commands to cultivate and to keep—but sometimes people transform the world according to their own desires.

To see how the definition works, let's now apply it to a simple tool, like our trusty shovel from chapter 2. The *activity* that we do with a shovel is moving dirt—literally an act of transforming God's creation. But typically people don't dig just for the sake of digging. They dig for some bigger purpose, or a *practical end*, such as building a house or burying treasure.

This brings us some additional distinctions that are sometimes helpful when talking about technology. The first is separating *tools* from the *products* of those tools. We can think of a tool as what we use to create something and a product as the thing we create or consume. For example, a camera is a tool because we use it to make something else, but a movie is a product because it is something we consume. A paintbrush is a tool for creating, but a painting is a product that we consume. A skillet is a tool to create an omelet, and the omelet itself is a product.

If we want to fulfill our calling to be God's creative image bearers, it's also important to distinguish between tools used to *create* products, tools used to *consume* products, and tools that both create and consume products. For example, a video camera is useful for creating a movie, while a television can only consume the movie. A computer, however, is good at both creating movies and consuming movies, and a fork can be used both to create and consume food.

So where do modern tools like mobile phones and social networks fit into these categories? They certainly have a practical end, but at first glance they don't really seem to transform God's creation—at least in a physical sense. However, these tools still have a powerful transformative effect on the world as we know it, something I observed firsthand during a recent trip to Oregon.

As a high school student, I was fortunate enough to have a dedicated youth group leader named Scott who took a few friends and me on hiking trips through the mountains of eastern Oregon every summer. Scott taught us how to purify water and cook our own food, but for us teenagers the best part was that we had no way of contacting our family for over a week.

Scott later organized a reunion for our group, taking us to the same places as adults we had been ten years before as teenagers. As I hiked in, I was amazed that the paths, lakes, trees, and mountains hadn't changed much since we had last visited. But it was after dinner that the transformation happened . . . when each of us reached into our packs and got out our phones. We ran around the campsite searching for a good signal, and once we found the "sweet spot," we called our wives and children to tell them about the hike. Those calls didn't transform God's creation in a literal sense like a shovel does, but the mobile phones still performed a very distinct transformative function.

On the surface, all a phone does is transport speech from here to there. But if we think differently about what's happening, the phone is transforming the physical and relational worlds by connecting two people who are physically distant. In addition, the presence of a phone in my pocket means that my conceptions of space, time, and limits are radically different than a world without phones. The mountains of eastern Oregon look the same as they did before phones, but the way I now experience them and the time with my friends has been transformed by our always-connected digital age.

While a phone only has the power to modify the limits of physical space, other communication technologies go a step further, transforming even time itself. When you make a voice or video call, you and another person have to operate your tools at the same time, but a tool like the book you are holding allows me to transfer thoughts and ideas to you without the need for both of us to do something at the same time. A phone allows us to have conversations across physical distances, but books allow us to have a conversation across time. In this sense, the technology of writing—whether in a book or on a website—transforms God's creation by shaping the way we experience both time and space.

Social media likewise has transformative effects on the way we experience the world by taking friendship and personal identity and reforming them into a unified, consistent experience. One of the first things we do when a new social media platform appears is take who we are and transform our identity into something that fits into its parameters. Different platforms prioritize different aspects of who we are, and the social conventions created around it reward different kinds of information. We will examine this idea more as we go, but the result is that in some sense *we* become the *product* of the *tool* of social media. We are not yet attempting to be critical of such tools, only pointing out that tools function as a cultural good, mediating certain values, meaning, and identity to us and those around us.

We now have a working definition of technology that encompasses everything from books and shovels to phones and drones: "The human activity of using tools to transform God's creation for practical purposes." Another simpler way of putting this is that technology is a "God-given transformative force." Creating and using technology is part of God's original command to create and cultivate the garden, which began with Adam's creation of language. This means that, theologically speaking, technology is good. But as we all know, Adam didn't stay in the garden for long, and we will now begin observing what happens when sin enters the world of technology.

QUESTIONS

- When you use the word *technology*, what are you typically referring to? How would you define it now and how might that affect how you use it in everyday life?
- What are some "social usage" patterns of technology that affect your life, relationships, and work?
- Do you use technology primarily to consume or to create? For entertainment or enrichment? Alone or with others?

5

REBELLION

THE FIRST AND LAST time I ever stole something I was ten years old. My mom dropped me off in the toy section in Walmart and said I could use my allowance to buy anything I wanted, but it turned out that I didn't bring enough money for both of the Teenage Mutant Ninja Turtle action figures I came for. So I bought one, but then while no one was looking, I went back and slipped a second one into my bag and casually walked away to find my mom.

I tried as hard as I could to act like nothing was out of the ordinary, but it was hard to contain the sense of exhilaration I felt as we pulled away from Walmart. However, the closer we got to my house, the more that feeling of exhilaration began transforming into guilt, worry, and regret. That evening I felt so sick I couldn't even eat dinner. I went back to my room to play with the toy I had so desperately wanted a few hours ago, only to find myself wishing that I could undo what I had done.

I imagine that Adam and Eve probably had a similar feeling in the moments after they finished eating the forbidden fruit. Those first few bites might've been pretty enjoyable, but as they neared the end, they would have realized something terrible had happened that could never be undone.

Now put yourself in Adam and Eve's position for a moment. You've just committed the world's first sin, introducing suffering and death to humanity. What would your first move be?

The First Technology?

If we turn on our phones and scroll to Genesis 3, we'll find that Adam and Eve's very first act after sinning simultaneously reflected their programming as God's image bearers and their newfound sinfulness. Genesis 3:7 says that as soon as they realized what they had done, their first response was to "make" something—their first set of clothing. (The text also says they "sewed" the leaves together, which makes one wonder if they already had invented some means of doing this prior to their sin.)

In the first few chapters of Genesis, there are several Hebrew words that describe God's creative acts. Sometimes he "creates,"[1] sometimes he "forms,"[2] and other times he "makes."[3] The most common is that last term, *make*, the same word used to describe what Adam and Eve did with the fig leaves. Even in their new sinful state, they didn't lose their status as God's image bearers, and it is almost as if they couldn't help but start creating.

Together, they transformed a bit of God's creation—fig leaves—into something with a practical purpose. In other words, they started doing technology according to the way we've defined it. Today we don't think of clothing as technology, but that's because we use it primarily to communicate fashion and status. For Adam and Eve, however, the fig leaves served a practical purpose—to protect them from their environment.

But like all human creations, their clothing was not limited to mere *function*. It also had meaning for them, and it represented the new values of their fallen state. Genesis tells us that in the moments after they ate the fruit, Adam and Eve suddenly became aware of their nakedness. Commentators suggest that on the surface this means just what it says—Adam and Eve recognized that they were literally nude. But the awareness of their physical nakedness also represents the knowledge that their sin was laid bare before a holy God.

Adam and Eve's clothing, then, was not only designed to protect them physically; it also represented their attempt to hide their spiritual broken-ness before God. Moreover, they were trying to invent a means by which they could live without God and were therefore acting in rebellion against him. Instead of living every day in a loving, open relationship with him—depending on his power and grace for their existence and joy—they tried to construct a world that would allow them to exist apart from him. The clothing was their way of transforming their circumstances such that they would no longer rely on God for anything.

The clothing also represents a major shift in their relationship with God and one another. From this point forward, Adam and his offspring would no longer walk with God in the garden. Instead, they would always com-municate with God *through* something else. It might be a dream, a voice, a book, a prophet, a burning bush, or even a donkey; but God's presence would always be mediated in some way. We were designed to experience the nonmediated (or *im*mediate) presence of God, but no human would experi-ence that again for generations.

In this first physical human invention, we find that technology can at the same time be both a reflection of the image of God and a subtle rebel-lion against him and his intentions for creation. Today every tool bears this double image, containing both the ability to reflect the goodness of God's creativity and the ability to perpetuate the myth that we can live apart from dependence upon God. Instead of affirming that the Son holds every speck of the universe in place, we amass tools with the belief that they can help us overcome our biggest problems and fulfill our deepest needs. Yet even though Adam and Eve clearly abused their creative powers, we'll soon find out that God didn't condemn them for their technological activity.

The First Technology Upgrade

As they were trying on their new clothes, Adam and Eve heard God walking toward them in the garden. As if hiding behind fig leaves weren't enough, they then tried to hide behind trees, hoping God would pass them by (Gen. 3:8). Of course this didn't work, and what follows is the sad announcement of God's judgment on creation.

Notice that God's curses directly interfere with the commands God had given in Genesis 1 and 2. God had called us to be "be fruitful and multiply," but now there would be pain in childbearing (3:16). God had called humanity to cultivate the earth, but now the ground was cursed, flawed, and broken (v. 17). From that point forward all of our creative acts and everything we make—even the most advanced of today's technology—will be built from sin-cursed material.

But Genesis 3 is not all bad news for technology. In fact, in the moments before Adam and Eve are kicked out of the garden, there is a bright spot. Before the angels with flaming swords arrive, God takes a look at Adam and Eve's garments, and instead of condemning the misuse of their creative powers and their attempt to solve their problems without him, God responds by doing something amazingly gracious—he gives out the world's first free technology upgrade. He replaces their rough, uncomfortable, and relatively small fig leaves with brand-new, state-of-the-art animal skins.

Genesis 3:21 says very matter-of-factly, "The LORD God made garments of skin for Adam and for his wife and clothed them." Again, the verb *make* shows up, the same one used when God "made" us in his image, when Adam and Eve "made" clothing, and now when the Creator "made" garments for his children. According to our definition of technology as transforming the natural world into useful things, God himself here is doing technology. Adam and Eve transformed fig leaves, but God transformed animal skins.[4] And in doing so, God appears to be sanctioning Adam and Eve's inventiveness, even offering them suggestions on how to improve upon it.

It is also significant that God's clothing upgrade comes just after he curses the environment but before he removes the fallen humans from the garden and sends them off into the harsh new wilderness. God's grace is evident in this because immediately after sin begins to take its toll on creation, God provides a means of lessening the effects of that curse.

Technology was originally part of our call to explore all of God's creation, but once sin appears in the world, technology takes on a new sense. Some of our technologies today can be understood as an attempt to overcome the effects of the fall. We can still build telescopes to explore the vastness of God's universe and new kitchen gadgets that help us try new flavor combinations. But we also make shovels and tractors to help us work the unruly land, and we invent epidurals to help ease the pain of childbearing. We build air conditioners and heaters to overcome the weather and frozen pizzas to overcome our hunger. We invent light bulbs to overcome the darkness, dating apps to overcome our loneliness, and search engines to overcome our lack of wisdom. Each of these inventions brings us incredible benefits, and collectively they are a God-given gift for reducing the suffering that we experience from the curses of the fall. A challenge for us is that the lines are sometimes murky between when technology is functioning according to God's original purpose, when it is overcoming an effect of the fall, and when it is an attempt to live sinfully or apart from God. We see these combined in Adam and Eve's clothing, which shows us that our technology alone cannot solve the deeper problem of sin that came with the fall.

This is why many theologians believe that in creating the animal-skin clothing, God was foreshadowing the means by which he would overcome the spiritual consequences of the fall. Adam and Eve tried to fix their sin problem with leaves, but God was giving them a visual picture of what the author of Hebrews would later write: "Without the shedding of blood there is no forgiveness" (Heb. 9:22). God was saying that no amount of technological activity—even when God himself is doing it—will ever fully overcome the curse of sin.

So God accomplished three things with the clothing he made. First, he affirmed that even after the fall, humanity is called to use its creativity to continue cultivating his creation. Even those of us who believe in total depravity—not that we are 100 percent bad, but that every aspect of our humanity is affected by sin—believe that the most sinful person among us is made in the image of God and that every creative act is a reflection of the One who imparted creativity to us. Christian or not, when a person creates a beautiful, functional device, she is reflecting the image of God. Second, God made it known that from time to time he will participate with humanity in doing technology. Sometimes he will help us ease the effects of the fall, and other times he will use technology more disruptively as a means of carrying out his plan of redemption. Finally, God was saying that while technology can temporarily ease some of our pain, we must not be so foolish as to make it our ultimate source of hope. We can and should use technology to ease suffering and aid in human flourishing, while also remembering that technology does not have the power to offer complete salvation and restoration. God alone will do that, and it will be quite costly for him.

The beautiful thing about technology is that it can offer us a foretaste of the coming kingdom of God. When we create better telescopes that show us more of God's creation, or 3D limbs that restore a person's ability to walk, our technological creations reflect back to his original creativity and forward to the redemption he is bringing. And yet we must be careful not to be seduced by the subtle lie that the right tools will enable us to live independent from our Creator, the sustainer of life. Medicine may help us live longer, but our bodies still need resurrection. Microphones might help us reach more people, but only a movement of God's Spirit can transform their soul. We must avoid the errors of two extremes, of saying either that this world doesn't matter or that this world is all that matters.

The deception of technological salvation that began with the fig leaves continues as we pick up the biblical story outside the garden, where we will find the deception growing ever stronger.

The Anti-gardener

Stepping into Genesis 4, we find that Adam and Eve are renewing God's plan to multiply and fill the earth, but also that the presence of sin would come to haunt their family. When their sons Cain and Abel brought their offerings before God, God approved of Abel's and rejected Cain's. This incensed Cain, and even after God warned him about the power of sin and temptation, Cain retaliated by killing his brother.

Interestingly, Genesis doesn't tell us why God rejected Cain's offering. The only difference comes in the content of their offerings—Cain brought crops, and Abel brought an animal. The laws of Israel allow both animal and plant offerings, so there isn't anything obviously wrong with what Cain brought. Abel is called "a keeper of sheep," but Cain gets the title "a worker of the ground" (Gen. 4:2 ESV), a direct reference to the words "man to work the ground" in Genesis 2:5. Cain, then, was doing word for word what God designed humanity to do on earth, and yet his sacrifice was rejected.

Thankfully, the author of Hebrews comes through again for us when he writes that the issue was not between crops and blood but between faith and faithlessness. He writes, "By faith Abel brought God a better offering than Cain did. By faith he was commended as righteous, when God spoke well of his offerings. And by faith Abel still speaks, even though he is dead" (Heb. 11:4). The apostle John also weighs in, using Cain as an example of doing evil when he writes, "Do not be like Cain, who belonged to the evil one and murdered his brother. And why did he murder him? Because his own actions were evil and his brother's were righteous" (1 John 3:12).

This situation teaches another lesson about creating and doing technology. Just as Adam and Eve showed that they could do technology for good even in their sinful state, Cain illustrates that we can do good technology in a faithless, sinful way. Cain was following the letter of the law when it came to the cultural mandate, and externally there was nothing wrong with what he made from the world. Yet John and Hebrews tell us God rejected Cain's work because it wasn't offered in faith.

Today we too can create helpful, productive, and even redemptive technology, but we still have a choice whether to offer it in faith as an act of worship or to do it for ourselves and our own glory. For example, I have created several tools that encourage Christians to read and study the Bible, but just because those tools are explicitly Christian doesn't mean my work is automatically worshipful or honoring to God. Likewise, if I build something like a video player, a food distribution system, or something else that we wouldn't normally label "Christian," that can still be offered as worship that honors God. And yet, as we've seen and continue to see, even when the posture of our creative activity is intended to glorify God, the things we make and use still sometimes have unintended effects. For example, Bible apps change how we read the Scriptures, and online church changes how we engage in community. So as we continue to consider our technology, we need to carefully consider both our own motives in making as well as the effects on ourselves and others as we use it.

The Anti-garden

Of course, Cain's story doesn't end with the killing of his brother. What he does next continues to be instructive for how we make technology, and what it means to us. After Abel's death, the discussion between Cain and God mirrors what happened between God and Cain's parents. First, God questions Cain, and like his parents, Cain makes excuses. Then God responds with curses, and Cain is forced to move even farther away from the garden. In Genesis 3:17, God told Adam, "*Cursed is the ground* because of you," but here God intensifies the curse, telling Cain, "*You are cursed* from the ground. . . . When you work the ground, it shall no longer yield to you its strength" (Gen. 4:11–12 ESV, emphases added). The ground is personified here, as God states that it will continually curse Cain. I can almost imagine Cain attempting to put a seed in the ground, and the ground spitting it back at him.

In Genesis 2, 3, and 4, the language of "cultivate the ground" is repeated over and over again, but with each successive sin the ability to do it is tainted and damaged, putting further distance between humanity and God's design. But God also puts literal distance between Cain and the ability to enjoy the bounty of creation. He tells Cain, "You shall be a restless wanderer on the earth" (Gen. 4:12). Cain had been designed to be at home in the garden, but God was now telling Cain that he would never have a home. Cain had been designed to have dominion over creation, but now the earth would dominate him. He was created to multiply and fill the earth, but instead he chose to reduce the human population. The consequences of his actions were that he had no brother, no friends, and no home.

So how does Cain respond to all of this? First, he negotiates with God to protect his life, and God, in his grace, offers to protect him. But then comes a curious little verse: "So Cain went out from the LORD's presence and lived in the land of Nod, east of Eden" (Gen. 4:16). Remember, God had placed angels with flaming swords on the east side of the garden of Eden (3:24), keeping Adam and Eve out. Now God forced Cain to go even farther east and farther away from the garden. In Hebrew the word *Nod* sounds like the word for "wanderer," and many commentators think that the "land of Nod" is a metaphor meant to portray Cain entering a state of wandering. The picture is that as he literally moved farther away from the garden, he was figuratively moving further away from God and who he was designed to be. He, like all of us in a sinful world, would never be able to return to his true home; and the more he sinned, the more physically and spiritually alienated he became.

But Cain was still a human being, designed to multiply and create. And in the next verse, we find that Cain did just that. Genesis 4:17 says that Cain and his wife had a child. But even more importantly, Cain did something that had never been done before—he "built a city." A well-designed city that balances cultivation and care could be considered the ultimate garden project, the natural result of ordering what God had made. And yet, under the influence of sin, we often misdirect our efforts away from the glory of God toward our own ends. As we've said before, our acts of making represent our values and identity, and Cain's city was no exception. It reflected what he wanted from the world and how he felt life should be.

The story of the first city also represents humanity's first expansion beyond individual tools to technological systems. The shift from nomadic hunter-gatherers to people who lived in a fixed location and raised cattle and planted crops allowed for increased human flourishing. But systems of power that can be used for good also allow for systemic evils and forms of oppression. In his book *The Meaning of the City*, theologian Jacques Ellul explores how the concept of the city is treated throughout the Bible. Ellul wrote that in building the first city, Cain was attempting to set up an alternative to the garden of Eden. Instead of a place where humans lived in relationship with God, deeply connected to him and his creation, Cain built a place where people could live without God and disconnect from his creation. In building his city, Cain collected as many tools and resources as he could find and attempted to create a place of safety and comfort, a place where he could be protected from the natural world and insulated from his need for God. Ellul writes:

> When man is faced with a curse he answers, "I'll take care of my problems." And he puts everything to work to become powerful, to keep the curse from having its effects. He creates the arts and the sciences, he raises an army, he constructs chariots, he builds cities. The spirit of might is a response to the divine curse.[5]

In building his city, Cain was obviously doing technology. He was using tools to transform God's creation for practical ends, and like his parents he both fulfilled his role as an image bearer while at the same time living in rebellion against God. Although the biblical story will ultimately culminate in God's creation of a redeemed heavenly city (Heb. 11:16; Rev. 21:1–2), Ellul points out that in many places, the Bible portrays cities as places of evil, disconnected from God and creation, where people use their creative powers to create systems of exploitive wealth rather than expansive justice. When Jesus addressed people, he offered blessings to some and curses to others, but when he mentioned cities, it was always in the context of judgment.

This is in part because the city is one of humankind's first idols. An idol doesn't have to be a golden statue; it can be anything that takes the place of God in our lives. We use our idols as a way of meeting our needs apart from God, and this is our greatest temptation with technology—to use it as a substitute for God.

The fifth-century theologian Augustine wrote that all sin is an incurvature of the soul, or a turning inward toward the self.[6] Technology, for all its good, often amplifies and augments this inward turn. In *The City of God*, Augustine goes on to say of the city that, "By craving to be more, man becomes less; and by aspiring to be self-[sufficient], he fell away from Him who is [truly sufficient for him]."[7]

We also use our idols, especially our technological ones, as a means of distraction. When we find something that offers us temporary relief from the curse of sin, instead of allowing its shortcomings to make us long for our Savior, we allow the technology to distract us from our obvious need of a savior. Blaise Pascal, the seventeenth-century philosopher and mathematician, captured our tendency toward distraction when he wrote, "When I have occasionally set myself to consider the different distractions of men . . . I have discovered that all the unhappiness of men arises from one single fact, that they cannot stay quietly in their own chamber."[8] Cain distracted himself with the tools of his day, and we distract ourselves with our ever-present televisions, constantly buzzing phones, and endless doomscrolling. From Cain's city to our modern electronics, we are constantly seeking something that will distract us from coming to terms with the fact that we are all inhabitants of the land of Nod.

It would be wrong to conclude from this that technology is evil (remember, it's a good part of God's world) or that cities are inherently wrong. After all, God is taking us on a journey from the garden to the city. But we are observing how the transforming power of technology, including the city, can be hijacked by sin. As we progress through the biblical story, we'll continue to see the theme of the city, but for now let's see what technological applications emerge from Cain and his descendants.

The First Technological Revolution

Long before the revolutions of gunpowder, the printing press, and the internet, Genesis 4 tells us the story of the first technological revolution. Here in the city that Cain built to escape God, the Bible tells us that there was a technological and cultural explosion. Cain continued having children, and we find that his grandchildren went on to develop three major strands of human culture: "Adah gave birth to Jabal; he was the father of those who live in tents and *raise livestock*. His brother's name was Jubal; he was the father of all who *play stringed instruments and pipes*. Zillah also had a son, Tubal-Cain, who *forged all kinds of tools* out of bronze and iron" (Gen. 4:20–22, emphasis added).

Incredibly, we see that Cain's offspring—those born in the anti-garden at the center of humankind's rejection of God—developed three things: (1) animal husbandry, (2) art and music, and (3) metal tools that broadly summarize human culture.[9] Even today, these three categories apply to how our society operates. We still have the mass production of food through the farming industry. We still make music, books, and other forms of art. And of course, we still make and use tools out of materials we find and purify.

Thankfully, Genesis 4 doesn't end with the evil line of Cain conquering all. Instead, it ends on a more redemptive note with the birth of Cain's brother Seth: "And Adam knew his wife again, and she bore a son and called his name Seth. . . . To Seth also a son was born, and he called his name Enosh. At that time people began to call upon the name of the LORD" (vv. 25–26 ESV). In direct contrast to Cain's descendants, all of whom rejected God and did everything they could to live apart from him, the line of Seth is portrayed as the first to formally worship God. Interestingly, the Bible doesn't tell us if Seth's descendants created anything or contributed to culture. All we know about them is that they called upon the name of God.

It's almost as if Genesis is trying to contrast technological and cultural development with righteousness. Cain and the tool-using, music-playing pagans are over there, while the simple, backwoods believers are over here. Does this mean that God is telling us to retreat from creating? Does the comparison of Cain and Seth suggest that we should stop using technology and focus more on our worship?

As we'll see in the coming chapters of Genesis, the answer to this question is definitely no. God will demonstrate that he still wants us to be creators of cultural goods and doers of technology. And yet, the stories of Cain, Abel, and Seth hammer home the point that any act of making divorced from faith is less than it could be. God cares much more about our faith and the genuineness of our worship than how high-tech we are. Sadly, I've often heard people criticize a church, saying, "That church is so behind technologically. It's almost sad!" But I think this passage suggests that God is more interested in our theology of worship than in our technology of worship.

That said, technology and culture do matter in the story of God. And as we move deeper into the Scriptures and watch God begin his redemptive program, we'll find that technology will often have a small but important role to play. For now, we can summarize what we've found by saying that even in a world tainted by sin, God not only approves of but even helps with our technological development. In the presence of evil and suffering, technology has taken on a new sense of being one of the ways we overcome the effects of the fall and offer glimpses of the world to come.

In a speech on creativity given in 1982, Steve Jobs said, "If you're gonna make connections which are innovative . . . you have to not have the same bag of experiences as everyone else does or else you're going to make the same connections [as everybody else], and then you won't be innovative, and then nobody will give you an award."[10] Jobs's point is that our unique life experiences bring value to the creative process. I think we can take this one step further and be encouraged that God can redeem the suffering we have endured and allow it to fuel the kinds of technology we create and use. There is no part of our life that God cannot turn into something that brings him glory and offers us portraits of the goodness that is still in our world.

At the same time, technology is also one of the chief means by which humans attempt to create a world without God. As our technology grows more and more powerful, the illusion of control becomes increasingly convincing. Today, our powers have grown to the point that in industrialized countries, we can go through our entire lives without perceiving the slightest physical need for God or other people.

But does all of this mean that technology itself is inherently evil? Does technology *cause* us to do sinful things, or is technology itself simply neutral? In the next chapter, we'll try to answer these questions. We will start with a trip to Austin, Texas.

QUESTIONS

- What are some technologies that are closer to God's original purpose for technology (to have dominion and cultivate the garden), and what are some technologies that are used primarily to overcome the effects of the fall?

- What technologies do you think have the most capacity to insulate us from our need for God?
- How can we speak carefully about the negatives of technology without beginning to think that technology is not a good gift from God?

6

APPROACH

Every spring thousands of musicians, artists, and technology companies head down to Austin, Texas, for the annual South by Southwest (SXSW) conference. SXSW began as a music festival that lived up to Austin's motto of "Keep Austin Weird," but later it added an event for film and then another for interactive media called SXSW Interactive. Since the mid-1990s, SXSW Interactive has been one of the go-to events for companies attempting to launch new websites and mobile devices.

One year, a few days after SXSW ended, a local Christian radio host decided to have listeners to call in and discuss how Christians should use and think about technology. The first caller was an older gentleman who talked excitedly about a new app his church was using that reinforced the application points from the pastor's sermon throughout the week. The caller said he initially thought the pastor was crazy for texting about his sermons, but after receiving a few of the daily messages, he found himself trying harder to apply the sermon through the week. Both he and the host were impressed that his church was so forward-thinking and creative in their use of technology.

However, the next caller, a mother of three teenagers, wasn't so excited about texting. She quickly rattled off several horror stories about sexting in the local school system. In one of those stories, a girl sent an explicit photo of herself to a friend, who then shared it with so many people in their school that the girl was forced to leave and start homeschooling. The caller then started to share other worries about how technology was affecting her own kids. She said her kids spent most of their evenings locked away in their rooms on their phones. Through the conversation it was obvious that technology was her enemy. "Technology is making my kids narcissistic!" she said in exasperation.

You've probably heard these kinds of back-and-forth conversations before. One person shares a story of technology making everything better, citing missionaries speeding translation work with technology and advances in medicine. But then another person counters with stories of pornography, affairs on social media, and how technology is destroying society and undermining traditional family values.

The radio program ended the way many such conversations do. A "wise person," in this case the radio host, tried to calm down the audience a bit, telling them that they needed to remember that technology itself is neither good nor evil. We can't blame technology for our problems, he said, because technology itself is simply neutral. What matters is that we try to use our technology in a way that glorifies God and furthers the gospel. As long as we aren't using technology for selfish purposes, then we can make it into a force for good.

After what we've seen in the Scriptures about technology, what do you think about what the radio host had to say? Is he right? How does his view square with God's original command to create culture, part of which is doing technology? And what about the city of Cain and humanity's attempts to live apart from God using technology?

Neutrality and Gray Areas

When I ask audiences if they believe technology is good, bad, or neutral, almost every time 90 percent of the audience will raise their hand to answer "neutral," echoing the view of the radio host. And there's good reason for that—it makes a lot of sense within a Christian view of the world. We believe that God is holy and that he wants our choices to line up with his design, so it is good for us to be concerned with issues of right and wrong. We also believe that inanimate objects like shovels and phones are not moral creatures, and we know that they cannot force us do anything. We alone, not machines, are responsible for our choices.

When we come across an activity that can't be clearly classified as morally good or morally bad, we put that activity in a special category called a "gray area." Into this category we put things like watching R-rated movies, getting tattoos, or voting for a certain party. Since we can't make universal statements about whether these choices are clearly black or white, we say that they are gray, and we tell individuals to take them up with God and their conscience.

By default, most of us think of technology as a gray area as well because a phone can be used for morally good or morally evil purposes, so we often categorize the device (and the choice to carry one) as "neutral." However, once we've decided that the device is neutral, we tend to ignore the device itself and focus only on what we use it for. We believe that as long as we use the phone to call good people and not to do something like arm a bomb on a plane, then we have nothing to worry about.

But is this really all we can say about technology? More importantly, is this all we *should* say about technology? While the viewpoint of our radio host is certainly well-meaning, I believe it short-circuits the kind of deeper discussion about technology that we must have in order to live faithfully in today's world. We have already seen that God calls our creativity "good" and that our technological creations are included. But for those who insist that technology is neutral, Marshall McLuhan has some strong words: "Our conventional response to all media, namely that it is how they are used that counts, is the numb stance of the technological idiot."[1] I'm guessing that none of us want to be idiots, especially not technological idiots, so we need to spend some time developing ways to talk about technology without falling into the trap of calling it neutral and limiting our discussion to how we should use it.

Philosophy of Technology 101

In his book *The Whale and the Reactor*, Langdon Winner wrote, "At this late date in the development of our industrial/technological civilization the most accurate observation to be made about the philosophy of technology is that there really isn't one."[2] But while Winner may be correct that there is not a single agreed-upon philosophy of technology, most people—including those who called in to the radio program—approach technology through a particular philosophy whether they realize it or not. In fact, the host and callers represented two distinct philosophies of technology that we will examine below. In the academic world, there are dozens of theories and finely nuanced viewpoints on technology, but they can be summarized into two extreme poles with several intermediate viewpoints somewhere in between.

At one end of the spectrum is *instrumentalism*, a view very similar to what the radio host unknowingly espoused and the view that I mentioned I held until my professor challenged me to think more carefully. Instrumentalism gets its name from the belief that technology is merely the instrument of the person using it. The tool itself is neutral in that it is interchangeable with any other tool with no effect.

Instrumentalism is often expressed in the popular notion that "guns don't kill people, people kill people." This pithy saying is arguing that guns should not receive any blame when one person kills another. The gun is simply the instrument the killer chose to use, but the killer could have exchanged it for any other weapon. Therefore, there is no need to worry about the presence or absences of guns, only how people use them.

This argument certainly has a ring of truth to it. People are in fact responsible for their actions, and societies put people in jail, not guns. Yet while clever and popular, this bumper sticker slogan doesn't tell the whole story about how guns and people interact. A question that can help us go deeper into the nature of technology is, Does this technology have values? In other words, what is it designed to do and what are the results? In the case of a gun, we might say it values "long-range, precise damage." Because of these inherent values in guns, we treat them differently than other objects of similar size and shape. For example, a home with a gun is a different place than one without a gun, because when we bring a gun into a home, we also bring with it a set of cultural practices (Kline's "technology as social practice" from chapter 4) that acknowledge its values. This includes rules like keeping the gun in a safe place, never pointing it at anyone, and only touching the trigger when you are ready to fire. These rules are essential for keeping everyone safe, but they also mean that even if the gun is never taken out of its case, the presence of a gun commands a different way of life than a life without guns. Sadly, even with such safeguards in place, we know that suicide rates are higher in homes with guns than in homes without guns.[3]

Remember, this example isn't meant to argue that guns are evil by nature, but to point out ways in which their presence cannot be described as neutral. And guns are not unique in this regard. In fact, every technology brings with it a set of values which leads to choices that alter the way we live. This line of thinking leads us to the view of technology at the opposite end of the spectrum from instrumentalism.

This second view, called *technological determinism*, says that technology is an unstoppable power that has become the driving force in society. While instrumentalism claims that technology has no inherent values, determinism focuses on another question: Do humans have agency? Determinism says no, essentially arguing that technology operates independently of human choices. Determinists go so far as to say that technology is the primary basis of and reason for societal and cultural change.

Determinism shows up popularly with this statement: "Technology *makes* us . . ." finished by blaming technology for some cultural ill. This was essentially what the callers who worried about technology were saying. But it's not just people who call in to radio programs that think this. Bookshelves have been filled with authors claiming that a certain technology, usually a more recent one, is responsible for just about every problem we have. The implication is that if we could just remove the technology, the problem would go away because technology *is* the problem.

But not all technological determinists see technology as a negative force. In fact, one of the most famous technological determinists, Karl Marx, wrote that technology would be the great force that equalized humanity. He is famous for saying that the windmill was responsible for eliminating the feudal system, and he believed that future technological advances might eliminate poverty and power altogether. Other determinists interpret technology as the primary means of perpetuating human evolution. Once our ancestors developed enough brain capacity to create tools, they no longer needed claws or long teeth. This allowed them to evolve even larger brains, which enabled them to develop more powerful tools, and so on. Some believe that biological evolution has stopped and that the next stage of humanity will come when we develop tools that enable us to escape the need for material bodies. These optimistic determinists tend to see technology as a force driving us in a net-positive direction, where pessimistic determinists often frame technology as the eventual downfall of human civilization.

Obviously, determinism won't do for Christians who believe that God, not technology, is the sovereign, driving force in history. But many philosophers of technology disagree with this view as well. MIT professor Leo Marx has written:

> We amplify the hazardous character of the concept by investing it with agency—by using the word technology as the subject of active verbs. Take, for example, a stock historical generalization such as: "the cotton-picking machine transformed the southern agricultural economy and set off the Great Migration of black farm workers to northern cities." Here we tacitly invest a machine with the power to initiate change, as if it were capable of altering the course of events, of history itself.[4]

This leads us to seek a middle-ground position on technology. We don't want to say that technology is inert or without values like the instrumentalists, and at the same time we don't want to claim that technology is responsible for everything like the determinists. Instead, we want to acknowledge that individuals and cultures interact with technology in a complex way. Both determinism and instrumentalism have elements of truth to them, but we cannot reduce all discussions about technology in either direction. People are culpable for their choices, but technology still plays a role in influencing the decisions they make. Below is a simple visualization of this continuum of thought, with instrumentalism at one end and determinism on the other. Naturally, we want to be somewhere in the middle, acknowledging both the values inherent in a technology and the choices we can make.

Instrumentalism	Critical Approach/ Christian Theology	Determinism
Technology has no values; humans are in complete control.	Technology has inherent values, and humans have choice and agency.	Technology is the driving force of society outside human control.

Values, Choices, and Culture

Let's look deeper into the question of technology and values, and how those change across cultures. When we talked about "cultivating the garden" in chapter 3, we said that the act of making things always results in an embedding of values and meaning into the things we make. When we use those things and perform cultural practices around them, they reflect back to us the values and meaning we assigned to them.

With some cultural goods like paintings, altars, and crucifixes, that meaning is explicit and by design. But with tools, the values are more implicit, arising from a problem we believe we need to solve. Most tools reflect the importance assigned to them by their maker, and the problems the maker wants to solve. When we buy and use a tool, we are participating in solving what our culture considers to be a problem in need of a solution. For example, a culture that hunts game for food will tend to invent weapons, and it will value members of their society who can run fast. But a culture that plants crops for food will invent plows, and those people will value strong men and women. The hunter culture will develop rituals around hunting and making weapons that reinforce their importance for survival, while the farmers will create rituals around their seasonal planting.

This same embedding of values took place in the mechanical revolution as well. For example, when people created cars, one of the reasons they did so was because they valued traveling. Traveling by horse and wagon was slow, and traveling by train was limited to specific routes. The car allowed the speed of the train and the individual routes of a wagon. Although none of the early automobile innovators probably thought about it, the car now has embedded in it the value of allowing an individual to travel wherever, whenever.

The independence offered by the car, however, was not equally received in all cultures. In the late 1800s, people in the United States were already known for having a strong individualistic identity, and the automobile served to reinforce that value. Eventually, the car would become for Americans both a symbol of and a means to freedom. This was especially true for American teens, for whom the car was the tool that could take them from the world their parents controlled to a world where they were free to be and do whatever they pleased. Since the 1950s, the ritual of getting a car has functioned in the same way that receiving a bow or a knife would have in many hunter-gatherer societies long ago.

If technological determinism were correct, we would assume that introducing a car into any culture would result in the same effect. But history tells a different story. When automobiles came to Europe, people there did not buy them at anywhere near the same rate as in America. The reasons for this are, of course, very complex, but it can be partially explained by the fact that Europeans have a different set of values, and so they treated the automobile differently. Perhaps because their cities were older and more historically rooted, the radical freedom offered by the automobile was not as attractive. This means that while technology contains in it the values of its makers, its users don't always react to those values in exactly the same way.

Another important factor to consider is that neither the makers nor early adopters of a tool know exactly what the tool will mean to the people who use it. For example, when mobile phones first appeared on the market, most people bought them "only for emergencies." They primarily considered cell phones in terms of their ability to allow a person to make a call from anywhere. We valued them for the safety and security they offered. But what we as a society didn't consider was that the phone brings with it the value of receiving a call from anyone at any time. The result is that as long as there are phones in our pockets, we are constantly connected to millions of other people who might call at any moment.

It has been said that when Steve Jobs created the first iPhone, he imagined it would only solve a few small problems and would therefore only be used a few times a day. Little did he know that the ecosystem of apps and notifications would value something very different than what he envisioned. We bought our phones because we valued solving one problem (safety) without realizing that the phone also brings with it the value of constant connection and interaction. Notifications are a technology that value getting our attention, but they do not guarantee that everything that gets our attention is truly valuable. We must be careful to exercise our agency to decide when and where we want to direct our attention.

The values inherent in a technology and the choices we make around them also affect our relationships. When we go for coffee with another person, the presence of phones brings an entirely new value system. In the days of dumb phones, we might inadvertently be saying that we value not only our friend's company but also the company of anyone else who might call. In the age of smartphones, however, the presence of a phone on the table often sends the message that we value the world "out there" as much or more as the person in front of us. We'd like to think this message is only sent when we actually check our phones as a person is talking, but studies have shown that when people are asked how they felt after a conversation, those who talked in a phone-free environment felt more fulfilled, while those who spoke with a phone visible (even if it didn't beep, buzz, or get touched) reported feeling more anxious and frustrated.[5] In a sense, this means that the back of the phone sends as strong of a message as the front of the phone.

If instrumentalism were true, then the presence of the phones shouldn't have an effect on our relationships, but experience tells us this is not true. On the other hand, if determinism were true, then we would have no choice as to whether we set our phone on the table or answer a call or have so many notifications turned on that we cannot resist the buzzing in our pockets. Somewhere in between these two views, we can acknowledge the values and priorities of the device while also remembering that we have choices about the way we use technology that will either reinforce our stated values or assume the values of the device.

Media Ecology 101

Philosophy of technology helps us think through the nature of technology, and media ecology is another area of study that introduces some helpful ideas for thinking about how media interact with one another and society. Marshall McLuhan introduced the term "media ecology" to help us think beyond individual devices and consider them in the larger human world of people, places, communication, and other devices.

Using this term was McLuhan's way of inviting us to think of media and technology as analogous to a biological ecosystem. In any given environment there is a careful balance of resources, predators, and prey, but when a new species is introduced into an environment, it affects all the other plants and animals in the system. For example, if you drop a shark into a fish tank, the shark won't simply be added alongside the other fish. Instead, there will be a major clash, changing the makeup and order of the fish tank.

Neil Postman, a student of McLuhan's, extended this analogy when he wrote, "Technology is ecological, not additive."[6] Postman was pointing out that new technology always changes the makeup of the technological ecosystem. For example, when television came into homes, it wasn't simply "additive" alongside radio. Instead, television changed our relationship with radio, how often we used it, and what we used it for.

In fact, the television and movie industries offer a great example of how media functions like an ecosystem. Earlier, we considered how technological change transformed the music industry as songs moved from live performances to recorded media to digital media and streaming. We can similarly trace the progression of home television technology, from the black-and-white boxes of the 1950s to the giant color sets of the '80s to flat-screen TVs. As screen tech advanced, several devices came along that we "added" to the

TV, starting with broadcast TV antenna and cable networks, progressing to content that could be played from physical media (VHS and DVDs), and then advancing to streaming services like Netflix and Disney+.

McLuhan's technological idiot would say that antennas, DVDs, and streaming platforms are themselves simply neutral tools. All that matters, this line of thinking tells us, is the content of the shows. This line of thinking tends to limit our focus to considering whether the images are pleasing to God, but causes us to ignore how the medium through which we access the images might also be forming our minds and hearts. Of course, it is important to consider the content we are consuming and how it honors God and our fellow image bearers. But a purely moralistic approach misses entirely what McLuhan and others are pointing out about the media we use to consume those images. If we consider each iteration of visual technology more carefully, we'll see that they not only made it easier to buy, watch, and record shows and movies, they also fundamentally changed our relationship to those shows and the kinds of content that get created.

In the era of broadcast TV, the episodes of a show tended to stand alone, and a person could watch them independently and in any order. The characters and the situation were the same, but there wasn't any overarching story across a season. This worked well when viewers could only watch shows at a set time every week or on reruns, because it didn't matter if you missed an episode. But as more and more tools for recording shows came along, TV creators began to experiment with more complex storylines. This was only possible because people could buy a season on DVD or record it on a DVR and catch up on what they had missed. This is an example of what Postman means by technology not being purely additive. Adding these recording technologies had an ecological effect on the nature of TV shows.

As with streaming music, streaming TV services also changed the way shows were consumed and produced. Instead of a season being released over a period of weeks and months, content creators experimented with releasing entire seasons all at once. This progression meant that TV shows began to function more like long, interconnected movies. At the same time, the movie industry began to experiment with creating interconnected movies, the most successful of which have been in the Marvel Cinematic Universe. Movies were becoming episodes of a TV show.

While the traditional categories of TV and movies were blurring, digital services, YouTube in particular, were enabling creative people not attached to a big media company to produce their own kind of content. From the short-form video sites to the longer-form content seen on YouTube, entire new genres have been created that are remixed and riffed on by others. Phones have made vertically oriented video possible and popular, which also influences the kind of content we create and consume. Together, all of these little changes mean that the media industry is a very different place than it was a several decades ago. We might be able to say that the technology used to consume content (radio, TV, streaming, etc.) is not *morally* good or bad, and yet these examples show why it isn't helpful or accurate to call these mediums "neutral." We don't want to err into determinism and argue that streaming services *made* anyone do anything, but neither do we want to err into instrumentalism and say that the change in medium didn't matter or had no effect. Instead, we need to remind ourselves not only that art itself (movies, shows, and music) is an important element of culture, but so also are the devices we use to consume them (TVs, laptops, phones). When our devices change, our culture changes, and then the things people do in our culture change as well.

Let's apply this concept of media environments to church and how the technologies around it affect our ecclesiology. Think back for a moment to what church life would have been like in the 1850s. A horse-drawn wagon would allow you to travel a maximum of five miles in an hour, so it would only be feasible to travel a few miles on Sunday morning. This meant that the number of churches you could choose from would be limited, and most congregations would be fairly small. But at the turn of the twentieth century, two big changes occurred. First, there was a migration from sparsely populated rural areas to dense urban environments. Second, the creation of the automobile allowed farther and faster travel. The combination of the presence of the automobile and the density of our cities resulted in a quite different set of choices about how and where we do church today. Yet none of us would claim that the choice of where we go to church is morally or spiritually neutral.

Cars changed *where* we go to church, but another technology changed *how* we do church. As urbanization and automobiles were spreading across America, evangelists like Billy Sunday and Billy Graham began holding rallies in stadiums employing a special new set of technologies—the microphone and the speaker. The stadiums and speakers allowed them to reach the huge audiences who drove to see them. In the 1950s, as these two technologies, the automobile and the microphone, made their way into churches, we began to see the rise of the first megachurches. Churches erected huge, stadium-like buildings and used speakers and video to reach the people who drove their cars from miles around to hear the latest popular speaker.

If we consider church as a kind of environment, media ecology would say that you cannot simply add technology with no effect. Instead, the new media will communicate a set of values and it will also present a new set of choices. Media ecologists often stress that new technology comes with a set of trade-offs that benefit some people more than others. For example, automobiles and microphones valued getting thousands of people in the same place on a Sunday morning, but that created a new problem. If we also value intimacy, relationships, and community, how can we do that in such a large setting? One solution was to break the people into smaller groups. Small groups were not a new concept in church life, but the 1950s megachurch offered a new spin: they tried to divide people into groups by age. Large churches today now have youth groups, college ministries, seniors groups, and so on. These can be wonderful places to learn and connect, and yet this division was a trade-off because it meant that younger and older people or people with different interests did not get to interact with and benefit from one another. The Word of God and the Spirit of God haven't changed, but when we change the God-given technologies we use to encounter and worship him, it has a transformative effect on that experience.

A Tool for Understanding Tools

In his later years, Marshall McLuhan offered what he called a technology tetrad that is helpful in teasing out some of the ways a new technology might affect us.[7] McLuhan's tetrad proposes that all media and technology do four things. First, they *extend* or *magnify* something that we do naturally. Microphones extend our voice, while telescopes magnify what our eyes can see. A phone is more complicated in that it extends more aspects of our humanity including not only our ability to communicate but also our sense of personal identity. Second, they *eliminate* or *amputate* something that we used to do. When we get used to using microphones, we tend not to develop the ability to project our voice. Phones seem to eradicate our ability to be unreachable and alone. Third, all media *retrieve* something from the past. Phones retrieve the ability to connect on a regular basis with a frequency and familiarity that people were accustomed to when they lived in small villages. Finally, every technology has the possibility to *reverse into* a more negative behavior when it's overused. When we use our phones too much, rather than deeply connect with people, we may maintain surface communication with the entire world.

McLuhan's four questions about media can be applied to any tool, from cars to TikTok, and going through the exercise can help us surface both the benefits and problems with technology. For example, a calculator *extends* our ability to do math, but it *amputates* the need to memorize multiplication tables. By doing math for us, the calculator *retrieves* time, yet when we use it too much, we *reverse into* not being able to do basic math ourselves. McLuhan's intent was not to demonize any of our tools, or to say that one was better than another, but only to help us recognize that technology is not neutral by uncovering some of the unexpected effects that come with using technology.

The Ends and Means Are Connected

Another way to think about the effects of changing one technology for another is to consider the connection between ends and means. The aphorism "the ends justify the means" argues that it doesn't matter what means you use; the only thing that matters is that you achieve the desired result (the ends). But we know that the means do matter deeply. We cannot use immoral ends to achieve a moral result. When it comes to technology, we cannot simply swap one for the other and expect to arrive at the same end.

Consider for a moment the means of travel used by missionaries. In the early 1800s, Christian missionaries got to their destination on a ship whose voyage could take several weeks or even months. But today, newly minted missionaries hop on a plane that takes them from one continent to another in less than twenty-four hours. The starting and ending points are exactly the same, but the technology obviously transforms the experience. A plane reduces the time it takes to travel from weeks to hours, but even more significant is the meaning of that time. The voyage at sea often functioned as a slow, gradual transition from one culture to the next as missionaries spent time with fellow passengers from both their native culture and the one to which they were traveling. Today's missionaries don't have this built-in transition time and must adjust at warp speed when their plane touches foreign soil. On the other hand, faster travel means that today's missionaries are able to take more frequent furloughs and share more of what God is doing through them with the people who support them back home.

The point is that changing the means always alters the ends. As we transition from one technology to another, we never arrive at exactly the same end point. As Christians, we often say, "the means change, but the message stays the same." However, while it's true that the gospel message never changes, the means by which that message is communicated does, in fact, bring with it additional ends.

One of the most important examples of this has been online church. The earliest recorded expression of an online church may have been as early as 1985, and there have been church services conducted through a variety of internet platforms since then. These online churches were primarily smaller experiments in new platforms, extensions of large media-heavy churches, or ministries to reach closed countries. But the global lockdowns of 2020 meant that nearly every Christian had an experience with a form of online church. This experience illustrated much of what we have explored here. First, if the end or goal of church is worship, we discovered that we cannot simply change the means from in-person to online without drastically changing the experience. We also saw that different technologies bring a different set of values. Churches that streamed their services through some type of video platform like YouTube or Facebook found that those tools allowed them to reach a maximum number of people on almost any device. But those that used videoconferencing tools like Zoom found that it valued interactivity and congregants seeing one another as well as the clergy. Virtual reality services, though still relatively rare, value a sense of space and location, and VR allows small groups of people to have conversations in ways that cannot happen with a grid of dozens of faces.

What these technologies do not, or rather cannot, value is being physically near to other humans. Some people use the word *disembodied* to describe online interaction in a negative way, but I don't think this is helpful because we are always embodied whether we are sitting on a pew in a church, standing at home with hands raised high next to a family member, or alone in a room with a VR headset. Instead, we need to pay more attention to the forms of embodiment different technologies allow and encourage, and how that is different from being physically nearby other people.

Using McLuhan's tetrad, we could say that an online service *extends* a church's ability to worship beyond the building and into the home. But we would also say that it *eliminates* our physical proximity from one another. In the case of a pandemic, staying apart was actually a desired end for health and safety. But just as John and Paul expressed longings to both write *and* be physically gathered, we too sensed that exclusively worshipping from home would not have been healthy in the long term (except in certain unique cases such as those who are infirm or who live in unsafe areas). We could also say that online church *recalls* a time of itinerant preachers, home churches, and smaller gatherings when large corporate gatherings were rare, but that it could *reverse into* isolationism or a lack of diverse, local community.

This kind of analysis helps us to validate the importance of online ministry, but it also reminds us that we cannot simply transfer what happens in a local church to the digital world without considering the values and ecological changes technology brings. We do not want to make the error of instrumentalism and say that technology doesn't matter, but neither do we want to assume that all technological change is negative and new technology should be avoided.

Technology and the Flesh

In previous chapters we have said that technology is a God-given good, and in this chapter we have explored some of the ways in which technology also brings with it unintended consequences. Adding to this complexity is the fact that we live in a world where sin taints everything. What the Scriptures call our "flesh" is that part of us that is always bent toward self, at the expense of others and the exclusion of God. Our flesh, then, will always gravitate toward technology that favors the individual over the group. When a technology has the built-in value of personal choice and exclusion of others, our flesh will want to capitalize upon that value. This goes all the way back to Cain, who used the technology of the city to insulate himself from God and his creation and to serve his own selfish motives. If we combine what we know about the flesh with McLuhan's idea that technology "amplifies" an aspect of our humanity, we find that technology can amplify the "incurvature of the soul" about which Augustine wrote. Jesus warned us that when we attach a mouth to our heart, bad things often come out (Luke 6:45; see also James 3:3–6). That sinfulness is amplified all the more when we attach something as powerful as the internet to our hearts.

Our task as believers is to work against the tendencies built into our devices that can feed the flesh, and, in effect, to become predators of the media in the ecosystem of our lives. Being a good predator means knowing one's prey well, and the more powerful the prey, the more careful we must be with it. For example, almost every social media platform has some way of tracking what is popular through tools such as likes, comments, and retweets. Humans tend to crave novelty, and when these two factors are combined, we find that social media tends to value posts and pictures that offer stimulation over reflection. Over the years we've now seen that social media tends to reward controversy, anger, and inanity over confession, contemplation, and kindness.[8] We still have a choice in how we use it, but to honor God and keep ourselves healthy, we must work against both the values of the technology and the disorder of our souls.

Today, successful technology companies are often not those that build good products but those that can exploit these human weaknesses. Likewise,

Christians who live God-honoring lives in the digital world are those who can discern the tendencies built into all technology and then decide when those tendencies are in line with godly values, and when those tendencies might be damaging to the soul. When we are aware of the tendencies and values inherent in our technology, we have the best chance of avoiding the negative trade-offs it brings and, instead, of using the technology to serve God. Technology creators too can work toward building things that promote and reward human flourishing over short-term gains and popularity.

In the next chapter, we'll return to the Scriptures, where we'll find God beginning his program to redeem humanity; but we might be surprised to find that God sometimes goes out of his way to give technology a place in the story, showing us how we can make and use technology for redemptive ends. To illustrate this, I want to tell you about a very interesting lab in Boston.

QUESTIONS

- When you think about technology, have you leaned toward ideas that sound like instrumentalism (technology is neutral; all that matters is how you use it) or determinism (technology is an overpowering force unalterably taking society in a direction)?

- Think through some examples of how changing the ends and means are connected. For example, if you want to share photos with family (ends), how does that change from mailing printed photos to emailing digital photos to sharing on social media (means)?

- Apply McLuhan's tetrad (media *extends*, *amputates*, *retrieves*, and *reverses into*) to a variety of technology (e.g., a drill, an airplane, streaming music). Does McLuhan's idea still hold up in the digital age?

- What are some areas of your flesh where you feel particularly pulled by what a technology values, and how can you resist that in community?

7

REDEMPTION

SEVERAL YEARS AGO, I had the privilege of meeting Dr. Rosalind Picard, the founder and director of the Affective Computing research group at the Massachusetts Institute of Technology Media Lab and founding faculty chair of MIT's MindHandHeart initiative. All those titles mean that she is one of the world's most experienced and impressive technologists, having published hundreds of articles on artificial intelligence and machine learning, received several patents for algorithms and sensors, and created a successful company around her research.

Picard pioneered the field of affective computing, which is the study and creation of technology that can both interpret and stimulate human affect, or emotion. One of her many projects was to train computers to recognize human facial reactions to different points in a conversation, such as furrowing a brow in confusion, nodding in recognition, looking off in boredom, or smiling at humor. This technology could have a variety of applications for computers and user interfaces, but one of Picard's primary applications for her research was to help humans, not machines. She wanted to use the technology to provide people on the autism spectrum, who often lack the ability to interpret facial expressions, with live feedback on how a conversation was going.

In a world where companies are trying to use facial recognition to sell more products, and where governments want to use it to control citizens, Picard is using technology and creativity in a restorative way. Part of the reason Picard directs her work in this way is that she grew up as an atheist but later became a Christian, and her faith has led her to advocate for the redemptive power of technology. She serves as a wonderful example to Christian creators and technology users everywhere of how to direct our image-bearing creative powers toward ends that honor God and fulfill the proper place of technology.

In prior chapters, we've seen that technology can serve both to reflect the creativity of God and rebel against him. Its original purpose was to cultivate the garden and explore God's creation, but, like all of creation, the presence of sin corrupted its purpose and meaning. In this chapter, we'll see a third aspect of technology: sometimes God uses the tendencies and value systems inherent in technology to move along his redemptive purposes. There are dozens of biblical stories that we simply don't have room to discuss (David's adoption of Hittite iron-smelting tools comes to mind), so we will limit our discussion to three familiar episodes: Noah's ark, the Tower of Babel, and the giving of the law to Moses.

Blueprints: Noah's Ark

Just before Adam and Eve left the garden, we saw God graciously upgrade their first act of technological creation by remaking their clothing with better materials. Obviously, the clothing could not fully restore them to their pre-fall state, but it did protect them from the harsh new world they were about to experience. In this sense, the tool of clothing offered Adam and Eve a form of redemption, albeit a temporary one. As we step out of the garden, we'll see that this was not the only time God chose to use technology in his redemptive work.

The first is the story of Noah's ark, a story usually relegated to teaching children about animals, rainbows, and God's graciousness. Biblical scholars also find other important themes and messages, but rarely if ever do we read Noah's story with technology in mind. And yet, Noah's ark-building project lines up quite well with our definition of technology as "the human activity of using tools to transform God's creation for practical ends."

Interestingly, the story of Noah in Genesis 5 begins with several callbacks to the garden. First, there is a restatement of the fact that God created male and female humans in his image and likeness. Then Scripture goes further, saying that Adam fathered children in his image and likeness. Even in this sin-cursed world where brothers kill one another, God's image—and the creativity therein—is still being passed down from generation to generation. When Noah is born, his father, Lamech, refers back to when God cursed the ground, saying he hoped Noah would be able to provide "comfort" (the name Noah is related to the Hebrew word for comfort) to those suffering from the effects of the fall and relieve the "painful toil of our hands" (v. 29). Lamech seems to view his son as a savior from the curse of the fall, and, as we all know, Noah was a deliverer in some sense—just not exactly the kind for which his father had hoped.

In Genesis 6, God was so deeply grieved by wickedness that he wanted to destroy every human along with the creation they were designed to cultivate and keep: "Behold! I will destroy them with the earth" (v. 13 ESV). Thankfully, Noah found favor in the eyes of God, and God decided that even in his act of destruction, he would provide a way to save the human race.

What comes next in the story is so familiar to us that it's difficult to step back and see how unexpected God's plan was. Keep in mind that this is the same God who later would send an angel of death, part the Red Sea for the Israelites, and stop the sun, so he could have saved Noah by any number of supernatural means. But in his wisdom, God chose to save humanity using a technology he designed himself. In the following verses, God actually gives Noah the exact blueprints for the tool he is to build, including precise measurements and materials:

Make yourself an ark of cypress wood; make rooms in it and coat it with pitch inside and out. This is how you are to build it: The ark is to be three hundred cubits long, fifty cubits wide and thirty cubits high. Make a roof for it, leaving below the roof an opening one cubit high all around. Put a door in the side of the ark and make lower, middle and upper decks. (Gen. 6:14–16)

Again, as this passage comes from one of the most well-known stories of the Bible, none of this feels out of the ordinary. But what's happening is not too far removed from a science fiction movie, the kind where a kid finds the blueprints to an alien technology that can save the world. But there's no alien here and no Hollywood special effects—this is the God of the universe telling Noah what kind of sealer to use on his boat. In what *should* come as a major surprise to us, it is through this human-made, God-designed ark—a technology created from the raw material of the earth—that humanity finds salvation from the floodwaters of God's wrath. God certainly didn't need the ark to save Noah and his family, but for some reason it was important for Noah to *make* it. Again we see that the word "make" (the same one used to describe Adam and Eve's clothing) shows up repeatedly in this chapter, and the chapter ends with the words, "Noah *made* all that God had commanded" (Gen. 6:22, my translation to clarify the word use).

When the floodwaters receded and Noah stepped out of the boat, it appeared that the human race would get a fresh start. God renewed his commands to be fruitful and multiply, and put in place the seeds of a formal government structure (Gen. 9:6) in hopes of preventing the kind of evil that was washed away in the great flood. Noah then planted a vineyard (v. 20), recalling images of the garden of Eden and symbolizing a reboot of sorts for humanity.

But even with this rebooting of the human race, Noah's ark did not eradicate the virus of human sin. Sin had infected those caught in the floodwaters as well as the passengers of the ark. Even the ship's captain, the hoped-for savior Noah, was a son of Adam. Almost immediately, we find that Noah's sons tainted the fruits of his vineyard, and instead of cultivating and keeping it for God's glory, they perverted it (Gen. 9:21–24). By the end of the story, it's clear that Noah wasn't the one who would offer the salvation for which Lamech had hoped.

And yet, in this story, God seems to go out of his way to make technology and human creativity part of his redemptive work. Of course, we wouldn't expect technology to be our final savior, but we do see that it can offer us relief from suffering and, in some cases, help us avoid death. Like the clothing God made in Eden, the ark temporarily protected humanity from some of the curses of the fall. But God didn't just use the ark to relieve physical ailments; he also used it to nurse along the human race, protecting them from judgment and taking the first steps in securing their redemption. So why did God use a technology of his own design rather than some other supernatural means as part of his redemptive strategy?

In the previous chapter, one of the things we learned about technology is that the means (the tool) and ends (the outcome) are always connected. God certainly knows this as well, which means that his choice of means is always deliberate and meaningful. Perhaps God is telling us that he values not just humanity but also the creations of humanity. The use of the ark seems to indicate that the physical world—and what we make with it—is so important to God that he often graciously chooses to use what we make in his plan of redemption. He doesn't *need* to use what we make, but apparently it pleases him to do so.

Noah's story also foreshadows the coming of the true savior, Jesus, the Son of God. Both Noah and Jesus were righteous men who delivered the human race by means of wooden creations, Noah on the ark and Jesus on the cross. The tools themselves are powerless to save us. They are not magical, and they have no command over sin and death. Yet God has seen fit to use them to bring about his redemptive purposes.

I think this should encourage us that for all the trade-offs and unintended consequences that technology brings, we too can employ technology for redemptive ends. Digging wells for clean water, offering medicine to the sick, and even sending encouraging emails work against the sin that entered the world at the fall and bring about the kind of human flourishing

God designed us to experience. And when we use technology in service of the mission of the church to make disciples, we are following God's lead in using technology as a part of his redemptive plans.

Yet we must also be careful to affirm that the redemptive capacity of technology is limited and temporary. Advances in technology can give us the illusion that it might someday overcome death, but this is a tragic and distracting lie. Clean water and ample medicine can only hold off death for so long—eventually death will find us all. Instead, we should view the redemptive capacities of technology as a temporary means of offering a hurting world a foretaste of the kingdom God is working toward. He used the ark to keep humanity going long enough to save us, and we too can think of technology as a way of pointing people to the God who loves them and wants to wipe away every tear permanently. God, of course, doesn't need our tools to accomplish his plans, but in his wisdom he has chosen to make them part of the story. In the next story, however, we'll see that God doesn't just work through technology—sometimes he works against the values we imbue it with.

Social Networking: The Tower of Babel

Long before today's social media, the Tower of Babel gave us a story about what happens when people join together around a technology. In Genesis 11, we find the human race again rejecting God's plans for them in favor of technological achievement. The story has several important echoes and contrasts with the previous story of the garden, Cain and Abel, and Noah, all addressing the importance of creativity, making, and human language. The story begins by introducing the idea of language and words (v. 1), echoing back to God's speaking the world into being with his word and Adam's task to name the animals in the garden. Then the people travel east and settled there (v. 2), reminding us of Adam and Eve being forced to go east of Eden (3:24) and that Cain settled with his family (4:16). In the next verses, the people of Babel conspire to "build" a tower (11:4), which is the same word used when God "fashioned" Eve from Adam's rib (2:22 NASB), Cain built his city (4:17), and Noah built an altar (8:20). And the process of using tar for mortar is similar to the way Noah covered the ark with pitch (6:14).

When God comes down to look at the tower the humans are building, he says that once they finish the tower, "nothing they plan to do will be impossible for them" (Gen. 11:6). This almost makes it sound like God was worried that the people of Babel were growing too powerful and that their creation would enable them to outstrip his control. But the word usually translated "do" in the sentence "nothing they plan to do" is the same Hebrew word as the one for "make" that we've seen throughout the first few chapters of Genesis, when Adam and Eve "make" clothing and Noah "made" the ark. God's concern is that the people of Babel were abusing their creative powers to derail his design for humanity.

Inherent in the technology of bricks are the values of strength, stability, and regularity, allowing people to build taller and safer structures than they could with most other materials. The people of Babel began to absorb these values, but rather than using their creative powers to honor God as Noah did, the people of Babel wanted to bring glory to themselves. Rather than live in dependence upon God (as Abraham will do in the coming chapters), they tried to achieve complete autonomy from him. Like Cain, the people of Babel saw technology as the means by which they could overcome the limits of a sinful world and remain independent of God. When God created the garden, he put humankind in it to reflect his image. At Babel, we find humans creating a city as their anti-garden and a tower as an image to themselves.

God's response to the tower is familiar to us, but if we take a moment to think about it from a fresh perspective, it is rather surprising. One might expect God to have simply leveled their tower and crushed the walls of their city as he did with Jericho. Instead, however, he chose to work at a more subtle and fundamental aspect of their lives—their language. As we saw in chapter 3, language is something that we create not only to communicate information but also to establish a sense of identity and inform the way we see the world. Many anthropologists say that if you truly want to learn about a people group, you need only to learn their language and it will tell you all you need to know. By confusing their languages, God was essentially reprogramming their sense of self, their relational connections, and how they viewed the world.

Though the story says God went to "confuse their language" (11:7), confusion was not God's ultimate goal. Instead, he was setting up a system that would force the people to spread out, thus inadvertently fulfilling the commandment to fill the earth. Again, God might have chosen any means of doing this, but he saw fit to use the technology of language as the means of scattering people. The people who deeply trusted technology to give them security and meaning had those very things stripped away from them by technological change. Notice that God was able to change their behavior, but he didn't have to take away their free will or destroy their creation to do so. All he had to do was introduce technological change.

There are three important things we should notice in the story of the Tower of Babel. The first is that God is again using technology to push humanity in a redemptive direction toward the purpose for which he created them. Sometimes God works through direct supernatural action, sometimes he works through people, but this story reminds us that sometimes God works through human creations. In the case of the ark, God used technology to protect humanity. But in the confusion of languages at Babel, God worked against the values of technology. A universal language has the built-in value of connecting a people with a single identity, and God chose to work against that value by breaking up their linguistic ties.

The second important truth in this story is that technology cannot be separated from the social world. Today much of our technology is personalized and focused on the individual's preferences, but in reality every technological choice we make takes place within the context of the larger human community. Moreover, technology that is designed to be socially oriented is particularly powerful in motivating large groups of people to do things. Since the advent of modern social media, we have seen political uprisings around the world, even here in the United States. People often do things in groups that they would not do as individuals, and a shared technology can powerfully reinforce this social dynamic. The Tower of Babel should remind us that social networks are not just toys—they are part of the most powerful technology in the world, forming humans for good and for ill.

Finally, what happened at Babel illustrates that a technological change always brings cultural change. Technology does not *make* people do anything, but it does alter the choices people have in front of them. God didn't force the people of Babel to move, but by changing their communication technology, he made it extremely difficult for them to choose to stay put. Even today, when we introduce technological change in our families, jobs, or churches, we too will face a different set of choices, limitations, and abilities. Each new tool has a series of strengths and weaknesses and a unique set of values, and these factors work in concert to shape our world and influence our choices. Perhaps no story illustrates this better than the exodus.

Tablet Revolution: Moses and Bezalel

The exodus story has so much to teach us about creativity, culture, languages, images, and technology, it could warrant an entire book. The story begins with several women conspiring against Pharaoh and the clever use of another waterborne creation to rescue God's deliverer, Moses. For several chapters, God demonstrates his miraculous and awful supernatural power as he breaks the Egyptians, parts the Red Sea, and gives the people manna, all in order to rescue his people from slavery and show them he was their God.

Then, beginning in Exodus 19, something amazing happens. Moses ascends to the top of Mount Sinai, and God begins to give him the first version of the law. Over the next several chapters, we find the Ten Commandments; the beginnings of the social, ethical, and governmental laws of Israel; the dates for national days of feasting; and a reiteration that the Hebrew people will soon inhabit the promised land. In this section, God also gives detailed instructions for the tabernacle and the ark of the covenant, including the metals the people were to use for altars and the fabric they were to use for the priests' robes.

This section culminates with something very special—the first time the Spirit of God fills a human being. It wasn't Abraham or Sarah, Moses or Miriam. Rather, in Exodus 31 we see God calling Bezalel and Oholiab, whom God has given the gift of making and craftsmanship (vv. 2–3, 6). They were to use their skill and the power of the Spirit to make the ark that would contain the signs of God's faithfulness to his people and the tabernacle where the people would worship. God planned out everything in meticulous detail, down to the kinds of threads, metals, stones, and other materials the Israelites were to use for each element. Bezalel was tasked with taking the abstract laws and ideas about God and making them into something visible and tangible, something a largely illiterate people could see and touch and smell and feel. God, through Moses and Bezalel, was giving the Hebrew people a set of objects, images, rituals, and language that would transform them into an entirely new culture, distinct from everyone around them. Some elements recalled the peace, wholeness, and intimacy of the garden of Eden; others, the reality and consequences of sin; and still others, the hope of redemption and restoration.

This new culture and way of life was important because the Hebrew people had been trapped in Egypt for four hundred years, and the only world they knew was slavery and pain and shame. As they ventured out into the desert, the people began to feel a sense of displacement and unfamiliarity. They were free, but they were also in uncertain territory, looking for something that could help them make sense of their new situation. Slavery was terrible, but when the pattern of their lives was disrupted, the people would often grumble and express a longing for the familiarity of Egypt.

Then, as they waited for Moses from Exodus 19–31, they finally lost patience. Exodus 32 tells the story of Aaron helping to craft the golden calf, Israel's disastrous replacement for the one true God. At this point in the story, we might be tempted to ask, Why in the world would they do something so obviously wrong? Everyone knows idols are offensive to God. But this story is about more than just literally creating statues to worship. Instead, what we see here is that humans long for the elements of culture we have been discussing. We want repetition and predictable patterns of life, symbols that give us meaning and anchor our lives. When we feel disconnected, disrupted, or displaced, we often reach out for things that will make sense of life, even if those things are destructive.

God knew that coming out of Egypt, a polytheistic society that personified their gods with statues, his people would need a new way of life, including cultural goods, artifacts, practices, and rituals that would ground them in the reality that they were his. God wanted his people to be "holy" or "set apart," and one of the best ways to do this was to give them an entirely new set of objects and rituals designed to communicate their identity as the people of God with the values of their Creator. They were to carry on the legacy of being God's image bearers, not make images of God using wood and metal. God was preparing what they needed, and he even assigned someone to build it, but, sadly, the Israelites couldn't wait just one more chapter.

As we live more of our lives online, many of us find ourselves in a kind of desert of meaning and connection. Devoid of healthy patterns and rituals, we often find ourselves drifting toward the ever-present call of our always-on devices. They are not idols in the sense of a golden statue that we worship, but they can become functionally indistinguishable when we cede to them the formative power of the primary patterns of our lives. This story is a warning not only to worship God alone, but also that we must work to develop healthy patterns of life and surround ourselves with the kind of language and imagery that will form us in the way of Jesus.

It Is Written

Having set the stage for why the giving of the law was so important, we can now focus on some additional aspects of the law, the first of which is simply that it was written down. Most Christian scholars believe that Moses and the Israelites crossed the Red Sea around 1444 BC, meaning that God would have carved out the first set of stone tablets around that time, and Moses would have written the remainder of the Pentateuch sometime after that.

What is fascinating about this is that when God wrote the Ten Commandments on stone tablets, alphabetical writing was still somewhat of a bleeding-edge technology. People had been speaking and using language since the days of Adam, but in Moses's day writing itself was still a fairly new concept. At some point in history, humans started creating cave art, and gradually those drawings morphed into the hieroglyphics that we see in ancient Egyptian tombs. Those hieroglyphics are often called pictograms because each drawing represents a word or a concept. Instead of characters like we have in our alphabet, a pictographic language can have thousands and thousands of symbols. This meant that hieroglyphics were a new, exciting way to share stories, but they weren't terribly efficient.

After a few centuries of using pictograms, someone decided that instead of using symbols to represent an idea or an object, symbols could be created to represent sounds. This was called a phonetic (sound-based) alphabet, and it is the basis of the alphabet we use today. Scholars debate the exact time frame and location of the first phonetic alphabet, but everyone agrees that it originated in the region of Canaan, Sinai, or Egypt between the nineteenth and fifteenth centuries BC.

The importance of these dates is that, during this time, the descendants of Jacob and Joseph were enslaved in Egypt. This means that the Hebrews were effectively living in the Silicon Valley of their day, watching one of the first major communication revolutions. Although they didn't create the first alphabet, early forms of Hebrew are directly related to those first alphabets.

This is significant because the technology of writing is one of the most powerful transformative agents one can introduce into a culture. Before writing, the only place to store information and ideas was in a person's mind. If you wanted to know something, the only way to get that information was to ask another human being. And if you wanted to get the most accurate data, you would naturally go see the oldest people in town, since it would be the elders of the community who would have accumulated the most information. In oral societies, before writing was invented, young people automatically looked up to their elders since they were the best and only source of knowledge.

Writing turned this social arrangement on its head because, for the first time, writing allowed knowledge to reside outside the human mind. Writing is so ancient that we no longer see it as a technology, but it was perhaps the most transformative of all the "extensions" of humanity because it was the first to extend the mind. Today, storing data outside our minds is an everyday occurrence as we store almost all of our knowledge on paper or computers. But before writing there was no such thing as to-do lists or spreadsheets. Any information that wasn't stored in the mind of a living person was inaccessible, and if a person died without verbally passing on this knowledge, the knowledge too would die.

The technology of writing meant that any person who could read had access to information that would normally take a lifetime to accumulate. No matter how young or old a person was, the one who could acquire the skill of decoding letters no longer needed other human beings to gain knowledge. A young person who had been educated could become a respected leader of the people.

This is just what happened with the transition in leadership from Moses to Joshua. The Bible tells us that God chose Joshua because of the faith he demonstrated when he trusted that God would give his people victory over the Canaanites. When Moses died, the technology of writing allowed Joshua to have access to Moses's knowledge of God and the commandments he laid out for Israel. Faith and righteousness were still requirements for spiritual leadership, but writing meant that age was no longer a necessary factor.

The technology of writing also has a set of values, notably permanence and authority. The spoken word tends to be fluid, and when we transfer ideas from one person to another, we often tend to introduce small changes over time. If you've ever played the game telephone, you know how quickly speech gets transformed when it travels from person to person. In contrast, the technology of writing values exactness and precision. By choosing this technology, God was communicating that his law did not contain optional truths or malleable commands. His law was literally set in stone.

In the early days of writing, writing was incredibly time-consuming and expensive. This meant that people could only afford to write down what was of the highest importance to them. Unlike our throwaway to-do lists, virtually everything written down was vital. This meant that when people invoked the words "It is written," they were appealing to the authority of the medium. After all, it wouldn't be written if it weren't important.

This means that God chose a medium of communication that was not only cutting edge for the time but also reinforced the message of that law. In creating the culture of the people of Israel, God was giving the world his final, authoritative, and unchanging law, and he chose a technological medium that reinforced those values. God, in his infinite wisdom, orchestrated the timing of the exodus so it would line up with the availability of the technology of writing, putting him at the forefront of technological usage. There is no wait-and-see policy—instead, God is always working through the tools of the day as he accomplishes his redemptive program. However, we ought not to conclude from this that God doesn't care about which tools we use. In fact, in the words of the law, we find that God did not limit his outlook to the medium of writing. He also had his eye on another powerful medium of communication and culture—the image.

The Importance of Images

When we think of the Old Testament world, we don't usually think of magazines, billboards, phones, and all the other ways we encounter images throughout the day. And yet, the Ten Commandments make a special point to address how formatively important images are. Let's read the first two commandments:

1. You shall have no other gods before me.
2. You shall not make for yourself a carved image. . . . You shall not bow down to them or serve them.[1]

The first commandment is the central defining theological truth that differentiated Israel from all cultures that surrounded it. The Hebrews were not to treat Yahweh as the highest god among the pantheon of other gods and goddesses. Instead, they were to be a nation of monotheists who worshipped Yahweh, the one true God, and Yahweh alone.

Then the very next commandment concerns the word that keeps popping up in our study of media and technology—"make." Before God said anything about murdering, stealing, or coveting, he gave the people of Israel guidelines referring back to the creation mandate from Genesis 1 and 2. The Hebrews were not free to approach God however they pleased, through whatever means they might find enlightening, fun, or interesting. Instead, God comes out of the gate with explicit commands on the relationship between their making and their worship.

When we compare the Ten Commandments to the ethical systems of other cultures around this time, many of them have commands that are reminiscent of "Thou shalt not murder" and "Thou shalt not steal." But these first two commandments are completely unique to anything found in the ancient world. No other ancient rule set commanded monotheism, and no other system puts such a high importance on the tools and objects used for worship. Neil Postman (who was himself of Jewish descent) noted this difference when he wrote, "It is a strange injunction to include as part of an ethical system [instructions on how they were to symbolize, or not symbolize, their experience] *unless its author assumed a connection between forms of human communication and the quality of a culture*."[2] An Israelite might have said, "What difference does it make if I create an idol to represent God, if I'm still worshipping Yahweh?" But in the second commandment, God is telling Israel that the images, forms, and tools through which we approach him do, in fact, matter to him.

Although God is restricting the use of a particular medium—carved images—he does so for a very important reason. It's not that God thinks images themselves are inherently evil. It's because he recognizes that tools of technology never function as neutral, inert instruments. Instead, the tools we use always bring with them values that shape the culture that uses them. An idol made of wood or metal communicates that people created their gods, that their gods can be contained in small objects, and that the gods are all alike. If Yahweh had allowed the Israelites to make images of him, it would have communicated that he was like every other god, just another god among gods. But by forbidding images of himself, God reinforced his identity as wholly other. He is not an idol among idols or an image among images—he is the one true God, infinite and uncontainable. We are created in his image, not him in ours. Therefore, God decreed that the people of Israel were to approach him exclusively through the names, metaphors, and ideas found in the permanent, authoritative words of Scripture. The medium was the message.

Ethical Redemptive Design

As we wrap up our brief review of significant events where God uses human creativity as part of his redemptive work, it is also worth considering that scattered throughout the Old Testament are additional ethical guidelines about how we should go about using our creative powers. As God modeled in Genesis 1, our creative processes should include careful and purposeful design along with limits that ensure it contributes to human flourishing. One small example of this is an obscure law that says, "When you build a new house, make a parapet around your roof so that you may not bring the guilt of bloodshed on your house if someone falls from the roof" (Deut. 22:8).

This seems to be saying that when we create, we must also consider and plan for how our creations will affect those around us. The law commanded the Israelites to include reasonable safety measures when building a house, and we could extend this to creating software, mining natural resources, or city planning. In each case, we are called to carefully balance the call to cultivate and care for God's creation, especially human life. Creating the fastest, cheapest product that maximizes profits over people is clearly not within the bounds of how God wants us to create. But even when we are not seeking to openly exploit people, we also have a responsibility to consider how our creations might be misused or generate unintended consequences. As finite creatures, we will never be able to anticipate every possible problem, but we can build a layer of care into what we do.

The law warns against creating tools and systems that can be used to exploit in subtler ways:

> Use honest scales and honest weights, an honest ephah and an honest hin. I am the LORD your God, who brought you out of Egypt. (Lev. 19:36)

The LORD detests dishonest scales,
> but accurate weights find favor with him. (Prov. 11:1)

This is one of the most often repeated commands in the Old Testament, found in the Law (Lev. 19:36; Deut. 25:13–15), the Writings (Prov. 11:1; 16:11; 20:10, 23), and the Prophets (Ezek. 45:10; Hos. 12:7; Amos 8:5; Mic. 6:11). In each case, God condemns creating a tool (in this case, a scale) that can be used in a systematic way for unjust gain. In Leviticus, God connects the need for honest, accountable systems to his liberation of the Israelites from slavery, showing just how important this rule is. A sword can kill a person, but a scale can cheat an entire city into poverty. Today, we need to extend this principle to the way we create software, especially AI-driven tools, and Christians may also need to advocate for laws that prevent exploitation and ensure a level of fairness. And yet, we must also recognize that in the rapidly changing digital age, ethics cannot simply take the form of principles and rules. Instead, we need to develop deep sources of wisdom and virtue that can guide us in new situations (which is difficult to do when we are distracted).[3]

This is but a brief glimpse of the riches of scriptural guidance on how we should make and use technology. The wonderful, surprising news is that it has become increasingly clear that God has chosen to allow technology and culture to play a role in his plan of redemption. In story after story, he has also made it clear that the things we make—technology included—matter to him, and that he can operate both through and against them. God has also shown us that the mediums we use to communicate, worship, and approach him are incredibly important. Throughout the Old Testament, there are echoes and hints that one day God himself will ultimately become the medium of our redemption, but until that day we need to spend time more fully exploring how technological mediums work. To do so, I'd like to introduce you to one of my favorite seminary professors.

QUESTIONS

- What technologies do you consider most redemptive today? What technologies are needed to reduce suffering?
- What rituals and patterns of your life do you feel are most healthy or unhealthy, and what role does technology play in shaping those patterns?
- What ethical guidelines do you have (or need) for the technologies you use or create? What laws do you think need to be in place to protect human flourishing?

8

MEDIUMS

In seminary I learned an important lesson about communication from one of my favorite professors, a hilarious South American man named Oscar Lopez. Dr. Lopez had a style all his own, and he loved a good suit with a colorful, sometimes outlandish tie. One day he came to class dressed nicely as usual and said that he was going to teach about how nonverbal communication could impact our evangelism efforts. He began by making a joke about his deep Spanish accent, but as he transitioned into teaching about communication theory, he did something that was unusual for him—he took off his suit coat and put it over the back of his chair. As he continued, he reached up to his neck and slowly pulled on his bright red tie. It's pretty common for people to loosen their tie in the Texas heat, but strangely, Dr. Lopez kept pulling on it until it came completely off.

Then he really surprised everyone when he started unbuttoning his dress shirt, revealing his white sleeveless shirt underneath. He kept on speaking as if this were perfectly normal, but my classmates started looking around at each other and wondering what in the world was happening. After he took his dress shirt completely off, he added it to the pile of clothes on his chair and asked us, "Do you know why I wear a suit and tie to class every day?"

The room was silent. No one knew what to say.

After a few moments, Dr. Lopez said, "Because if I came into class looking like this, you'd think I was a gardener!"

Again, the room was silent. None of us wanted to laugh at a joke with racial undertones, but here in front of us was an older man of Latino descent wearing a white sleeveless undershirt, which in the South is the stereotypical dress code for a person who works outdoors. Dr. Lopez, of course, found our squeamishness hilarious, and after letting the awkwardness linger for several very long seconds, he burst into laughter, saying, "You seminary students are so serious!"

He then put his shirt back on and started to recite some of the ideas that we've all heard about the art of speaking, such as, "Ninety percent of communication is tone of voice." But he went on to say that it's not just tone of voice that affects how people interpret what we say. A variety of other factors affect communication, including accent, gender, race, and so on. In a sense, any time we're speaking to someone, we are taking the ideas in our minds and wrapping them in elements of who we are as a person. We then hand that entire package to the person listening, and their reaction is composed of what they think of both the words and the packaging.

This means that there is no such thing as pure communication. Put another way, all communication is mediated, whether through a written letter, a strong accent, or a nice dress. Even when we're not using technology, we constantly interpret the words people say based on nonverbal factors of the speaker. For example, Americans often assume a speaker with a British accent is more refined and intelligent than an American speaker, but British people have their own hierarchy of accents when they speak to one another. Studies show that we adapt our accent to people we like, and we listen more attentively to attractive people, but conversely, we take the opinions of people we find unattractive more seriously. Sometimes the same item will communicate different things in different contexts. A suit, for example, might communicate confidence and professionalism in a job interview but elitism and stuffiness to another group of people.

We could go on making these kinds of observations, but the general point is that communication is about more than just words. Words always come with packaging, and that packaging always brings with it its own message. If this is true regarding aspects of our personal identity such as our gender, accent, and choice of clothing, and if part of our calling as Christians is to communicate the truth of the gospel, then it's also important for us to pay careful attention to the way our words are mediated through the form of technology we unsurprisingly call mediums.

What Is a Medium?

When we move from communicating verbally to communicating through a tool or device, we are, in effect, rewrapping our words in a new set of packaging. Instead of mediating our words through elements of our identity, we are enveloping them in the identity, values, and meaning inherent in the particular technology we choose. We call those packages—whether it is an email, a handwritten note, a phone call, a social media post, or any other tool we use to communicate—*mediums*. The *message* is the content we transmit from our minds to our audience, while everything that surrounds those words can be considered a *medium*. If *culture* encompasses all of what we make of the world, and *technology* is a subset of culture making, then a *medium* is a specific form of communication technology (which could be an older physical *tool* or a modern digital *device*) that transmits (and transforms) a *message*.

There is, however, quite a bit of overlap in these terms. For example, the first landline phones were simple mediums that transmitted voices across long distances. But on modern smartphones, a person can choose from an almost infinite number of apps, only some of which are used for communicating. Similarly, there is a complex dynamic between language, technology, and mediums as they interact with one another, and in the following pages, I will sometimes use terms like "medium" and "communication technology" nearly synonymously to bring out different nuances in the discussion. There is also an overlap with mediums that are less technological in nature, such as art mediums like painting and sculpture. The commonality between all mediums is that they offer a means of communication between two or more parties, and that both the message and the medium interact and affect one another and their audiences.

This is why when God communicated the *message* of the law, he did so conscious not just of his words but also of the *medium* through which those words came. When he wanted his messages to be understood in different ways, he used other media, communicating his mystery and power through the burning bush (Exod. 3:2–3) and the ridiculousness of the hearer through a talking donkey (Num. 22:22–40). These examples hint that mediation is a significant part of the story of God and something to which we should give our attention.

Over time, humans have improved reading and writing technology, then added audio and visual mediums, and today we continue to create tools for live interaction. Each new tool, from handwritten letters and phone calls to social media and virtual reality, extends and mimics different human abilities. As we think through different tools, here are some questions that can help us break down how they work and what it means:

- *Form*: What forms of communication does the medium favor: text, audio, video, all three, or something more?
- *Posture*: Is this a one-way medium used primarily for consumption (a book or TV show) or a two-way medium for interaction? Is the method of response the same (texting, calling) or entirely different (liking, commenting)?
- *Time*: Is there a delay between messages (sending an email, writing an article) or does it work synchronously (phone call)?
- *Space*: Does it attempt to represent space (virtual reality), or does it flatten everyone (squares on video conference)?
- *Identity*: How does it represent the sender (text description, photograph, avatar, live video) and his or her presence?
- *Transaction*: Who is paying for the medium (you or advertisers) and what are their motivations?

As we think through the mediums we use, we will see mediums and, more broadly, all technology, do at least three things: they communicate meaning, they change relationships and cultures, and they shape our patterns of thinking and behaving.

Mediums Communicate Meaning

I recently signed up for two new online services, and the companies' responses demonstrated a basic principle of communication. When I paid for the first service, the company immediately emailed a receipt to me and then followed up with an email a few days later thanking me for my business. When I signed up for the second service, they too sent me a receipt, but a few days later I found a handwritten thank-you note from them in the mail. I double-checked it, thinking it might be a printed letter designed to look handwritten, but it turned out to be the real thing. The thank-you email from the first company and the thank-you letter from the second contained almost identical wording, but I found that my reaction to them was quite different. This wasn't because of *what* they said, but because of *how* they said it, the medium they chose to say it with.

This is a fairly dramatic example, but every medium brings with it some kind of meaning that is tied to its functionality. The characteristics of the technology and the way it works tend to shape how we understand and perceive the messages we send and receive.

Formality. The features and functionality of each medium invite different levels of formality. For example, the difference between a phone call and a text message is not just about hearing a voice versus reading a screen; it is also about the cadence of the social interaction. A phone call must be accepted while a text message comes in automatically. A phone call allows all parties to talk at the same time, while each text message happens one at a time. The phone call has a clear beginning and end, while each text message just happens. Because of these technical differences, we usually begin a phone call with a greeting, like "Hello, how are you?" and end it with a closing, like "Talk to you later."[1] Text messages don't require us to do either of these things because there is no defined beginning or ending to a text message. In the days of home phones shared by a family, another layer of conversation was required, such as, "Is DeAndre there?" But the direct access of a text allows us to send something unexpectedly hilarious in the middle of the day.

These examples tell us something very simple, and yet very important, about mediums. In general, newer communication technology requires fewer steps, and therefore there are fewer social conventions required for its use. When there are more built-in social conventions around using a medium, we tend to treat it more formally, and what we communicate tends to be more significant (as in letter writing). Conversely, when a newer technology removes the need for these social conventions, it also removes the sense of formality (as in a text message). But sometimes when a technology advances, such as the shift from voice-only calls to video calls, we introduce new social conventions and expectations because the medium more fully represents an in-person interaction.

Difficulty. The act of getting dressed and traveling to see a friend and the act of physically carrying a letter to a mailbox are both more difficult than a quick email that can be sent immediately with much less effort. This difference in difficulty is part of the reason older mediums tend to communicate a deeper sense of meaning and value than newer mediums do. For example, the handwritten note from the second company in the example above seemed more meaningful to me in part because I knew it took more effort for them to do. Similarly, if a girl tells her boyfriend, "I think we should date other people," he will perceive those words differently if she says them in person, via text message, or on social media. He will likely be disappointed by the message no matter how she delivers it, but something with more effort might at least soften the blow.

When we look around at other social conventions, we find that we almost always use older cultural goods when we want to signify that something is important. Wedding ceremonies usually involve older styles of clothing— tuxedos and long, beautiful gowns—to make the statement that this is a significant event. If a couple wants to make a date special, they forgo driving their car around downtown in favor of hiring a horse and buggy to take them on that same path. The older technology conveys the meaning that this is a significant event and may reinforce the identity of the couple.

Speed. The ease and speed of newer mediums enables incredible things, but it also allows us to send messages that we would not have sent given more time for reflection. We've all sent a text, email, or tweet that we later wish we could pull back. But using a newer, faster medium doesn't always communicate that the message is less significant. In certain cases, the speed of a newer medium heightens the significance of a message. For example, if a person attending a sporting event sends the score of a game to another person not in attendance, that message will obviously be more significant if it is sent in real time with a text than if it were sent via regular mail arriving days later. If a college admissions counselor sends a prospective student a text telling her that she's been accepted to the university, the use of texting might communicate that the university understands her generation and how they prefer to communicate.

Representation. It is also important to consider how the medium we are using represents us and the people we are interacting with. Ivan Illich, former Roman Catholic priest and technology critic, puts it this way: "Tools are intrinsic to social relationships. An individual relates himself in action to his society through the use of tools that he actively masters, or by which he is passively acted upon. To the degree that he masters his tools, he can invest the world with his meaning; to the degree that he is mastered by his tools, the shape of the tool determines his own self-image."[2]

For example, text-based tools only represent our thoughts but not our tone or facial expression. Phone calls only represent our voice but not our physicality. Zoom, FaceTime, and other videoconferencing tools show more of us, but they don't currently allow for true eye contact. Résumés, social media platforms, and websites each allow us to present a version of ourselves to the world that we feel is appropriate for the medium. Each of these tools makes new things possible and also makes some things impossible. For example, videoconferencing values and makes possible long-distance, face-to-face interaction, but when we are using a video-conferencing device, other forms of personal engagement like handshakes become impossible. In terms of meaning, a videoconference-based educational experience communicates at least two things: that this education is so valuable that it should be available remotely, and that live interaction is a key component of learning. At the same time, it could have the side effect of saying that in-person experiences are not important for learning.

A basic understanding of the different value systems built into each medium is important because if we want to love ourselves and our neighbor well, we need to be able to understand how we are participating in their formation not only by what we say but also through the mediums we use. It's also important to be aware that, depending on a person's age and familiarity with a medium, he or she might not resonate with what I've just said about formality, difficulty, and speed, and this brings up a second and perhaps even more important truth about mediums. Mediums not only communicate meaning; they also tend to create, divide, and reshape cultures.

Mediums Create Culture (and Cultural Divides)

Back in chapter 1, I quoted Douglas Adams saying that our reaction to technology can be divided into three time spans: (1) everything before you were born is just "stuff," (2) everything invented between birth and the age of thirty is wonderful, and (3) everything invented after you turn thirty will bring about the death of society. Why is it that people sometimes treat technology (and mediums) this way? Part of the reason is that, as we've said, language, culture, and technology are bound together very tightly, and any change in the way we communicate results in a change to our culture and way of life. People over thirty have spent their entire lives learning one pattern of communication, and when new communication tools and mediums come along, they disrupt these patterns.

This doesn't mean that all older people are technologically inept, or that all younger people are automatically able to use any new medium or social platform. In general, it does mean that when a person encounters a technology later in life, he or she may not adapt to it as quickly. Educator Marc Prensky coined the terms "digital natives" and "digital immigrants" to describe this divide.[3] Digital natives grow up with technology, and the use of technology becomes ingrained in the way these individuals think and go about life. But digital immigrants are always learning and playing catch-up, like an adult learning a second language.

The generation that grew up with TVs were a little slower to pick up home computers; those that had computers took time to adapt to the internet; those that grew up with the internet were still surprised when their kids started using phones; and even those who grew up in the digital age are surprised when the next generation uses a new medium or social platform differently than they do. We've experienced this in our own home, such as when my wife and I were leaving for a dinner date and she told our then-middle-school-aged kids, "No internet while we're gone." When we returned, they told us about a fun video call they had with some friends, and we were immediately disappointed. Why had they used the internet when we told them not to? It turns out they thought "the internet" meant looking at websites. For them, video calls were just a normal part of being a kid. Like us, many parents, even those who think of themselves as technologically knowledgeable, often struggle to keep up with the constant release of new platforms and new mediums through which their kids want to communicate. On each new app or platform, new styles of communication, humor, and response are created, each of which generates unique subcultures.

In a sense, this means that right now, in households all over the globe, there are people from several different cultures. Depending on when a person first uses various communication technologies, they may understand those mediums differently. Thankfully, these kinds of cultural divisions don't have to lead to negative experiences. Children and parents can help each other adjust to cultural changes, and with patience they can understand one another. Older and younger pastors can work together to understand the whole of their congregations and how to communicate the gospel to them. However, this doesn't always happen, and the techno-cultural divide between parents and children—and the older and younger groups in a congregation—often becomes a major source of conflict.

Outside of family or church dynamics, we've also seen how social media platforms can function like a language in that users tend to form cultures and conventions around a given app. The trends change so fast that it is nearly impossible to track or document what goes viral on a particular platform. Sometimes a particular subculture or age group will gravitate to one app or another, and other times, as an app grows in popularity and size, subcultures form within that app. These subcultures are reinforced by the algorithms that show users the content they most strongly respond to. This can create "filter bubbles" where users only hear from like-minded people, more deeply entrenching them in a particular subculture with its values and beliefs. This echo-chamber phenomenon has also allowed the proliferation of fake news and conspiracy theories where something that is demonstrably false can seem true because everyone in an algorithmic subculture believes it and reinforces it back to one another.

These cultural movements built on social media often disrupt traditional forms of authority, and scholars of digital religion have traced similar disruptions in the realm of religious authority. Heidi Campbell, for example, has traced the ways in which "digital religious creatives" (people who combine technical skill and religious work) can wield a high degree of power and influence within their church or ministry.[4] Digital media has also allowed religious authority to be created outside of traditional churches and ministries. Many Christian celebrity influencers start with offline authority and extend that to the internet, but others have generated their popularity entirely online by understanding and utilizing the trends of new platforms.

Each new tool comes with the ability to communicate different kinds of meaning and to create a new culture intimately familiar with its use. People in that new culture will see the world in a slightly different way, not only because they communicate through different mediums but because they think differently. This is because in addition to creating culture, mediums also shape the way we think and behave.

Mediums Shape Thinking and Behavior

Author and priest Tish Warren Harrison has written that "we are shaped every day, whether we know it or not, by practices—rituals and liturgies that make us who we are."[5] She is pointing out that whatever we do repeatedly tends to shape us. As we discussed earlier in the example of gym equipment, our bodies are remarkably adaptable, and we can choose to mold them by repeating a task over and over with an exercise machine.

It turns out that the same thing is true in the way our minds adapt to the mediums we use repeatedly. The more we use a technology that engages our minds, the more our minds adapt to the patterns (or liturgies) embedded in it. Professional photographers become so good at using their cameras that they develop the ability to see the world as if through the camera. They can visualize images the rest of us don't see. Similarly, for musicians, their instrument becomes an extension of them as they learn to think and feel through the way it sounds. If cameras and pianos literally change the way we see and hear the world, other mediums also present us with distinct ways of thinking and behaving in the world.

In the remainder of this chapter, we'll reflect on two older technologies—the printing press and photography—each of which has brought major shifts in the way we think about and see the world. We will then use our observations to continue our consideration of the digital age.

Printing Press. Although Chinese and Korean innovators invented movable type centuries before, Johannes Gutenberg is credited as the first to introduce the printing press in Europe in 1440. The new technology made producing books and disseminating information much easier, faster, and cheaper, and as we've said, the medium itself carried an innate message: information should be freed from authoritarian control. This led to major cultural shifts including the scientific revolution, the Protestant Reformation, and the creation of democratic nations like the United States. This new level of access to information also brought with it radical new ways of thinking embedded in the medium itself.

Before the printing press, books were hand copied, resulting in minor variations from copy to copy. But the printing press allowed for the creation of books that were completely uniform. Every letter was rendered with precision, and every page of every copy of every book looked exactly the same. As more people encountered print books, the medium began to encourage things like uniformity, accuracy, and complex linear thoughts. It turns out these are features of the scientific revolution as well as much of the theological work that followed it. Throughout church history, we find church leaders like Origen, Augustine, Hildegard of Bingen, and Thomas Aquinas working to organize the theology found throughout the Scriptures in a systematic way. But those thinkers were also comfortable with finding allegorical and metaphorical meanings in the biblical stories. However, as more printed books became available, literacy began to spread, which gave way to an emphasis on "literal" interpretation. By the time of Martin Luther and John Calvin, allegorical interpretation was largely looked down upon, and in the centuries that followed, theology became more and more science-like until systematic theology became nearly the only way of doing theology.[6]

Another way the Bible itself became more science-like and bookish was the invention of chapter and verse numbers, like Leviticus 3:16 or Ephesians 2:8–9. We have become so accustomed to those little numbers that it's hard to imagine they weren't part of the original inspired text. Each book of the Bible was simply one long block of text divided into paragraphs, much like this book. Various chapter systems had been developed in the 1200s, but it was during the 1550s, when the print era was in full swing, that scholars created the full-fledged chapter and verse numbering system we know today and began including it in published editions of the Bible.[7]

The new numbering system made it much easier for theologians to refer to passages of Scripture in a consistent manner. But by adding the chapter and verse numbers, they had in a sense effectively systematized the Scripture itself. Today, whenever we open a printed or app version of the Bible, we see the Word of God through this layer of technology, and we often interpret and understand the Scriptures according to this technological way of thinking. When we talk about our "life verse," support our theological position with a string of references, or hold up signs at sporting events (such as John 3:16), Scripture is being mediated through the innovation of the chapter and verse numbering system.

As we've said before, technology is the means by which we transform what God has made, and the communication technology of the printed Bible—with its versification system—fits that definition very well. Verse numbers literally reshape the text of Scripture and, subsequently, the thinking of the one who reads it. Verse numbers were created as a means to navigate Scripture quickly, but because means and ends are always connected, the means of verse numbers has brought with it the end of thinking about the Bible as a book of verses, which are easy to take out of context, disconnected from the flow of the book. For example, digital religion researchers have found that on social media, people are more likely to share verses that are therapeutically encouraging over those that grapple with subjects like sin and judgment, showing another powerful connection between various mediums.[8] Of course, I don't mean to imply that chapter and verse numbers are morally wrong—on the contrary, they are extremely helpful, and I am grateful for them. However, we must recognize that these technologies, from printed books to verse numbers, are never neutral. Instead, they, like all other technology, are value-laden, and as we use them, our minds adapt to their way of thinking.

Photography. Photography became more common around 1850, and it brings an entirely different set of values and way of mediating the world to us. When we read a printed book, we often forget that we are spending a lot of our mental energy converting letters into words, and then forming those words into sentences, concepts, and ideas. This is a skill that we learn in school and perfect with years of practice. But when we look at a picture, no translation is necessary. We are born with all the tools we need to understand images. There are certainly cultural differences in the way we interpret facial expressions, color, and so on, but this happens without a cultural context, without the need to learn a skill like reading text.

Shane Hipps, in his book *Flickering Pixels*, points out that the old adage "A picture is worth a thousand words" isn't really accurate. "It would seem a picture is actually worth a thousand emotions."[9] He gives the example of the difference between our reactions to a printed sentence like "The boy is sad" and a picture of a starving child, crying in the middle of a scorched desert. The printed sentence presents us with a logical, linear, abstract concept, but the picture immediately pulls on our hearts and draws us into a story. When we see words, they cause us to think; but when we see a picture, we react first and then think about our reaction afterward.

The power that images have to draw us into a story and evoke an emotional response can be seen in the way advertisers use images to associate positive emotions with the product they sell. In chapter 2 we said that advertising taps into the way humans understand the world through storytelling. Here we can take that a step deeper by noticing how visual mediums can be used to connect a product to something that elicits a strong emotional response (e.g., a cute baby, a beautiful woman, an image of power), creating an unconscious association in our minds between the feeling and the product. Before photography was common, advertising mostly consisted of a text-based list of features with line-drawings of a product. But today, advertisers focus less on features and more on feeling. Car commercials don't just inform you about their seating capacity; the commercial shows you happy, powerful, and good-looking people sitting in those seats. And the commercial invites you to *picture* or *visualize* yourself in the driver's seat, perhaps attracting a happy, powerful, and sexy person beside you. Every commercial for every product uses the power of images to link that product to emotions of happiness, power, and even sexual allure.

Photography also allowed a new behavior—you and I can look at a human without that person being able to look back at us. Though this was possible to some extent with a painting, photography brought it to the masses similar to the way the printing press made books widely available. In person, if we look at someone too long, they might notice us staring, and if they make eye contact, we look away in embarrassment. But photography invites us to *gaze*, to pore over every feature and flaw of a person, to experience their beauty and power and humanity without shame. This, like all our making, is a gift that has powerful consequences. The ability to capture the essence of a child before they grow up, to marvel at an athlete's raw capacity, or to remember the face of a loved one who is now gone are wonderful aspects of this technology. At the same time, we know photos and videos can be used for evil, to capture private things that should never be recorded. But before we think about those explicitly immoral uses of images, let us return to the word *gaze*. The pattern of looking at a person that cannot look back enables a kind of gaze that can turn that human being into an object. Rather than viewing that person as made in the image of God, we can begin to look at the picture for our own pleasure. When we form the habit of looking at images this way, as objects, that repeated pattern can begin to inform the way we look at people in the flesh. The term "male gaze" was created to describe a pattern of looking at and depicting women primarily as sexual objects for the pleasure of men.

This happens in advertisements where marketers tap into the powerful physical and emotional forces behind human sexuality, using it to tie those feelings to the products they are selling. This gaze is most explicit in the epidemic of pornography. It has been said that pornography has always been at the forefront of every communication technology, from printed books to early photography to the battle between VHS and Beta, and it continues to drive new forms of digital media, including the ones we carry around every day. As philosopher of science Justin E. H. Smith has written, "Our work machines and our porn machines are now *the same machines*."[10] But the power of pornography is not just its ability to distribute sexually explicit images that become a substitute for what God intends for sex. The allure of pornography is also built into the medium itself, to the way the images powerfully affect the emotions and seem to offer temporary relief from the hurts, pressures, and pains of life. Staying away from pornography then is not only a matter of knowing that the content is sinful and often horrifically exploitative, but also of understanding how the medium of images works upon the mind, heart, and soul.[11]

Internet. The internet brings together several of these previous technologies into something totally new, amazing, and sometimes frustrating. Like the printing press five hundred years before, the internet has extended our abilities by making it easier for anyone to publish and access information. We can ask our smart speaker just about anything and it will return an instant answer. There is good and bad content we can access, but also important is how our minds are shaped and amputated by accessing information through the web. For example, with equal access to all the world's information, we tend to cultivate the skill of searching for and accessing information rather than acquiring information, committing it to memory, and allowing it to shape our minds and hearts. Tim Challies writes, "As we increasingly dedicate ourselves to the pursuit of information, we grow increasingly unable or unwilling to distinguish between knowledge and information."[12] Developing deep wisdom as suggested in Scripture requires internalizing truth and meditating upon it, not merely having access to it. This process often takes place over a long period of time in the context of community, which is quite different from finding a quick answer online.

Moreover, when we spend all of our time scanning and accessing information, we often find ourselves suffering from information overload. But this is not just a feeling we have about too much data. Scientists at Temple University have shown that when we surround ourselves with many different pieces of information, our prefrontal cortex (the part of our brain that makes decisions) simply shuts off. Information is often helpful in making good decisions, but "with too much information people's decisions make less and less sense."[13] More recently, this has taken the form of many people having difficulty in discerning what is true online. Life and reality are often complex and nuanced with no quick, easy answers, and in that context, people will sometimes gravitate to a wild conspiracy that offers a simple explanation for what is happening in the world.

This is made possible in part by the way we read on screens. Books tend to be read word by word and line by line. Once a book is in our hands, we can't do much else with it, so we usually follow through with the act of reading. But when we read on a screen, we are almost always doing so in the context of looking for information. Our tendency is to scan headings and paragraphs looking for elements of interest, not to read word by word and line by line. If a page is not interesting or relevant, most people move on very quickly. This is why clickbait articles with outlandish or provocative titles often get more attention than carefully thought-out ones.

Over time, as we cultivate the skill of scanning screens, many of us now find it more difficult to read a book or even an article all the way through. Like a marathon runner who can't bench-press three hundred pounds, or a person who can bench-press three hundred pounds but can't run a marathon, we seem to cultivate either the skill of deep reading or the skill of scanning. It's possible to do both, but it is difficult to maintain both abilities. In an interview on PBS's show *Charlie Rose*, Google's then-CEO Eric Schmidt publicly worried about the effect this kind of reading—and the internet as a whole—has:

> I worry that the level of interrupt, the sort of overwhelming rapidity of information—and especially of stressful information—is in fact affecting cognition. It is in fact affecting deeper thinking. I still believe that sitting down and reading a book is the best way to really learn something. And I worry that we're losing that.[14]

Schmidt's concern leads us to another factor that dominates our digital lives: interruption. Most of our tools are designed to inform us when important information is available. Our phones constantly vibrate or beep when we receive notifications throughout the day. Computers alert us when software updates are available, when our batteries run low, when we've misspelled a word, and on and on. Device and app makers make more money when we use them, so they are incentivized not to make your life better but to create notifications to get you to return to the screen as often as possible. In a study from way back in 2004, researchers found that information workers were interrupted to switch tasks on average every three minutes.[15] This allows little time for workers to get into "the zone," and it can also affect our in-person connection. Decades later, the problem of deep focus and creativity has gotten worse, not better.

One reason why these issues are important to reflect upon is that a good portion of the Christian life requires the ability to concentrate and focus on ideas and people over long periods of time. Jesus is often seen retreating to silence and prayer (Luke 5:16; 6:12; 9:18, 28; 11:1; 22:41), but a life surrounded by screens and constant connection offers little opportunity to do this. Cardinal Robert Sarah writes:

> Our world no longer hears God because it is constantly speaking, at a devastating speed and volume, in order to say nothing. Modern civilization does not know how to be quiet. It holds forth in an unending monologue. . . . This age detests the things that silence brings us to: encounter, wonder, and kneeling before God.[16]

Spiritual depth requires the ability to pray for more than a few minutes, to memorize and meditate on Scripture (not search for it online), and to love God with our hearts *and* our minds. This means that we must be careful to cultivate and retain the skill of deeply reading and sincerely contemplating the things of God, something that attention-getting technologies do not value. Faithfulness also requires that we can sit with a person and deeply listen without being distracted by a phone or wearable. There may be no greater Christian witness in our time than someone who can truly master the art of listening well in an age of constant interruptions.

Digital. As it has grown and evolved, the internet and the devices we use to connect with it are no longer merely an information provider but an important and unescapable part of our social lives. In this sense, the digital world isn't so much a place we go; it's part of our everyday reality, and we constantly move back and forth between the digital world and the physical world. The word *digital* can encompass many kinds of technology, including those that help us write software, automate mundane tasks, or create new forms of art. Those can also be thought of as a "medium," but here we will limit ourselves to thinking about the patterns of thinking and behaving embedded in more interactive digital mediums, using social media as an example here (and VR in chapter 11).

It may seem obvious, but it's worth carefully pondering what social media lets us do and how it compares to other forms of social engagement. Without getting platform specific, there are generally three things we can do on almost any app: post, respond, or consume. If we consider the pattern of consumption on a social feed to the pattern of consumption on a printed newspaper or a blog, it's not hard to notice how the medium, the message, and the method of consumption are linked. Social media can track how you engage and offer you new material related to your interests, while other forms of media require some level of choice and navigation. It's always worth asking, "Why is this in my feed?"

This brings us to what may be the biggest and most important difference between social media and most prior forms of technology and media— that most social platforms are free services financed by advertising. This is summed up by the saying "If something is free, you are the product," which means that advertisers pay social media companies in order to access your personal information, send you customized ads, and attempt to influence your behavior (buying, voting, and so on). Below, we will analyze how communicating via social media influences our messages and relationships, but underneath the unique features of each platform is a common business model where keeping your attention and learning about you is what makes money.

In the early days of the internet, many people asked, "Is online community *real* community?" Today we no longer ask that question because we know that online interaction *is* real. It can be life-giving, awe-inspiring, and lol-causing as well as pain-inducing, anger-causing, and anxiety-provoking. The better question is, "What are the rules of the medium and what are the underlying messages and patterns that emerge from those rules?" If the question of the early internet was "Is the relationship real?" the question of the social internet is, "Is the transaction clear?" The answer to the first question is "yes," but the answer to the second question is almost always "no." Whenever a new social service comes online, we have to ask ourselves not just "What does it do?" but "Who is paying for it?" and "What do they want from me?" Even the most dedicated Christian will likely spend only a few hours a week in formal Christian discipleship, but they will spend many more hours on social media being discipled by advertisers on what to think and what is valuable. I'm wording this strongly not because I think everyone should give up all social media (though some should), but in order to warn us that being "in the world but not of the world" (a phrase drawn from John 15:19 and 17:14–16) is incredibly difficult with these forces at play.

Now let's move on to what we typically do on social media and the patterns of behavior and thought built into them. The most basic functionality is to post something, such as text, video, or images. There is also some functionality to respond using the same functionality or added functions such as a like, share, retweet, or other means of indicating approval or disapproval of what was posted. These features allow for many-layered discourse and complex discussion, but notice that there is no way to just show up and be. Some platforms have an "online" status indicator, but for the most part, one needs to post in order for another person to respond. Matthew Anderson writes, "We cannot simply *be* online and influence others like we can be in a concert hall or with a friend and have influence. . . . [Online presence requires a person to] act intentionally in some way . . . through writing comments or linking or posting a video response."[17] This means that social media platforms value expression and response over presence.

The pressure of "I post, therefore I exist" can form us in undesirable and unhealthy ways. A study conducted by the Girl Scouts of America found that 74 percent of girls surveyed said that other girls use social networking sites to seem "cooler than they really are." Girls who said they have low self-esteem were more likely than other girls to portray themselves as "sexy" or "crazy" in their profile.[18] Children with low self-esteem have always found ways to act out, but never before have they been connected to so many others who might take advantage of them. Even those of us who try not to intentionally portray ourselves differently online can easily forget that when we go online, we are in some sense *Alone Together*, as the title of MIT professor Sherry Turkle's book suggests.[19]

Finding people online who share our rare interests can be incredibly rewarding and life-giving. So also can keeping up with what friends are up to by checking in on what they post and say and do. Blogger and web developer Leisa Reichelt uses the term "ambient intimacy" to describe this background connection. She writes, "Ambient intimacy is about being able to keep in touch with people with a level of regularity and intimacy that you wouldn't usually have access to, because time and space conspire to make it impossible."[20] The Industrial Revolution created a world where we are no longer able to see our friends regularly, but online tools allow us to restore some of the day-to-day connection we've lost. As Sigmund Freud wrote almost a century ago, "If there had been no railway to conquer distance, my child would never have left town and I should need no telephone to hear his voice."[21]

As we learn the patterns of the system, we find that certain types of content tend to gain the most attention and response. We might find that funny pictures or provocative videos get more likes or that expressing a viewpoint with strong and witty language gets more response. As our minds begin to adapt to these patterns, we become more skilled in them the more feedback we receive. This can, in turn, begin to influence how we see the world. The more we use social platforms, the more we can find ourselves thinking about events throughout the day in terms of how post-worthy they might be, rather than reflecting on the meaning of our lives. If we use our phones to snap and post a picture of an important event, and that post gets a lot of feedback, then the next time we experience something important, we pull our phones out without thinking. This pattern of behavior can be considered a "liturgy" or "ritual" that shapes and reinterprets our lives. As Mark Sayers has written,

> In our world of platform and social networking, we all too easily fall into the danger of being more concerned with our audience than our inner world. Our inner world remains unhealed and undeveloped because we never truly experience withdrawal. There is no room for reflection and privacy. Instead we prepare each thought, action, and experience for broadcast.[22]

Unfortunately, some corners of social media have become largely about "pointing out a problem." Social media tends to reward the loudest voices who write in the most extreme terms, and even those who have legitimate issues to discuss find themselves falling into a system of angry posts and flame wars. It can sometimes be difficult to find the line between speaking prophetically for justice and simply repeating the issue of the day, standing up for a cause, or virtue signaling. Online activism and speaking out for truth are important, but they should lead us to action in the world beyond declarations of right and wrong. These are, of course, just a small sample of the opportunities and challenges of faithfully embracing technology in the digital age.

Before we move on, I want to consider one more way digital mediums are shaping our world in subtle but important ways. We don't always consider video platforms like YouTube to be social media, but YouTube is one of the highest trafficked sites on the internet. Most Christian discourse on it focuses on the morality of the content. However, if we look beneath the content, we will find ways its pattern of engagement does more subtle things, such as spawning countless subcultures and genres and influencing many areas of our lives, including the way we learn. For example, traditional learning starts with foundational knowledge and then builds up to application. But today, when someone needs to fix their sink, they don't take a fluid dynamics class first. They just search for what's wrong and watch until they find a solution. This "working backwards" way of learning is now influencing all levels of education. Twenty years ago, my seminary students might have wanted to spend more time on abstract theological ideas, and I had to push them to think about why it matters. But today, I love that students are eager to get right to the application of a text; however, I sometimes have to remind them to do the theological work too. Of course, I can't say this is entirely due to YouTube or other platforms, but it does illustrate another way our media can reshape the way we look at and respond to the world. And yet, this new approach to learning that YouTube and other video platforms enable with their infinite content and never-ending rabbit trails is also what enables the spread of dangerous misinformation. An early hope of the internet was that it would make information free such that anyone could access the truth, but we now realize that digital media also allows the creation of entire false worlds. A piece of false information ("The earth is flat") doesn't usually have much power on its own, but when it exists in an ecosystem of interconnected digital worlds (The Flat Earth Society), it can feel convincing for someone looking for an alternative. Sadly, this can happen with medicine, politics, and even the gospel.

Our goal here is not to denigrate digital media, the social internet, or virtual reality. What we are exploring is the way mediation works in non-neutral ways, both in person and through technological mediums. Beyond the information we are trying to convey, our bodies, tone of voice, and especially our technology shape and transform the messages we are sending, as well as our culture, thinking, and even behavior. And sometimes an act of mediation can contain a powerful theological truth.

The Image of the Invisible God

We have seen that God has used a variety of different forms of mediation to communicate to his beloved children, from an audible voice to a flaming bush to the written word. We have even seen that God restricted the use of carved images in Israelite worship in order to communicate that he was not like other gods who could be contained by a block of wood. But when God wanted to communicate the depth of his love and grace, he chose the ultimate medium: the eternal Son of God became a son of man.

The historical, embodied person of Jesus, a baby boy born in Bethlehem who grew to be a man, had on his lips a message of good news: the gospel. But as we have been saying, the medium is the message. Jesus himself is the good news. His incarnate presence communicates meaning ("God so loved the world," John 3:16), it creates new culture ("They will know you by your love"; see John 13:35), and it shapes thinking and behavior ("Do not conform to the pattern of this world, but be transformed by the renewing of your mind," Rom. 12:2).

The Scriptures say Jesus is both "the Word" (John 1:1) and "the image of the invisible God" (Col. 1:15), but the early church wondered how this related to the second-commandment prohibition about not making images of God. If God became flesh, was it permissible to make images representing Jesus? For several centuries, Christians debated this issue (now called the Iconoclast Controversy), holding several councils that went back and forth on the use of icons[23] in worship. In the end, a final council concluded that icons of Jesus could in fact be used in Christian worship. Their reasoning was that the act of making an image of Jesus is a kind of replaying of the incarnation. To them, images of Jesus were a theological reinforcement of the fact that the Son of God took on human form. The great theologian of that era, John of Damascus, wrote:

> When the Invisible One becomes visible to flesh then you may then draw a likeness of His form. When He who is a pure spirit, without form or limit, immeasurable in the boundlessness of His own nature, existing as God, takes upon Himself the form of a servant in substance and in stature, and a body of flesh, then you may draw His likeness, and show it to anyone willing to contemplate it.[24]

This means that because of the Incarnation, even when someone makes an image of Jesus with profane content, the medium itself still betrays the truth that God took on human form. This event means that Jesus can serve as the "mediator between God and mankind" (1 Tim. 2:5). Here we see a restatement of the good news, the gospel that God is restoring his kingdom by sending his Son as a medium to us and for us, who then offers us his Spirit as a constant guide and advocate. Not only does this help us appreciate God's presence through his Son and by his Spirit, it also means that if this is central to the biblical story, mediums and mediation should be something we take very seriously. The more carefully we consider the values and patterns inherent in the mediums we use, the better equipped we will be to share the gospel in both word and deed.

In the next chapter, we will continue our journey through the biblical story, looking more deeply into Christ's first coming and his own relationship to technology. We will also explore his second coming and see what role, if any, technology has in the new heavens and new earth that God has promised.

- Match the activities on the left to the medium on the right. Which medium should you choose and why?

Activities	Mediums
Decide where to eat	In person
Share address	Text
Brainstorm on a project	Email
Apologize to church	Video conference
Hire an employee	Social media post
Therapy session	Phone call
Confront a sin	Virtual reality
Encourage a friend	Hand-written note

- What differences have you observed in the way different generations or cultural groups understand certain mediums?
- Considering the idea that "If something is free, you are the product," who is funding the technologies you use most often?
- Do you primarily use media to *consume*, *create*, or *communicate*? If you could create an ideal medium, what would it be like?

9

RESTORATION

As we continue in the biblical story, we now transition from the promise of a Messiah in the Old Testament to the coming of Jesus and his promise to return again to restore all things. Augustine wrote, "The New Testament is hidden in the Old, the Old is made clear by the New."[1] One of the things the New Testament makes clear about the Old is that when God spoke the world into existence and his spirit hovered over the waters (Gen. 1:1–2), the second person of the Trinity, the eternal Son, was also present and active in the story of creation. Paul writes, "For in him all things were created: things in heaven and on earth, visible and invisible" (Col. 1:16). What we will find in this chapter is not only that Christ offers us the free gift of salvation and the chance to participate with him in establishing his kingdom on earth, but also that his incarnate life models the proper place of technology in our life.

The Gospel of John portrays the incarnation with the words, "The Word became flesh and made his dwelling among us" (1:14). Theologically speaking, "became flesh" means that the eternally begotten Son took on a human nature alongside his divine nature. That's a pretty big concept to grasp, so

John also offers us a more understandable metaphor related to creativity and making. The word translated in English as "made his dwelling" in the Greek is literally "tabernacled" or "pitched a tent." In other words, the Son of God made a dwelling—a human body—in order to become the Son of Man and come near to us. Even more fascinating is that in this human tabernacle, Jesus was also a creator and user of technology, a person who used tools to transform the natural world for practical purposes. But even more importantly, Jesus's interactions with certain human creations—the cross and the city—serve as a metaphor for understanding the powerful transformation that he is in the process of completing. After we've looked at this promised restoration, we will assemble what we've learned into something we can use to faithfully examine any technology and decide how or if to use it.

Jesus, the Technologist and Transformer

Sometime after Jesus began his public ministry preaching the gospel and validating his message with miracles, he returned to Nazareth where he grew up. When he began preaching, some people were astonished, and they asked, "Isn't this the carpenter's son?" (Matt. 13:55; see also Mark 6:3). Interestingly, the word translated "carpenter" here is the Greek word *tektōn*, which is related to our English term "technology." As we saw in chapter 4, *tektōn* meant "artisan" or "skilled worker" in Jesus's day, and tradition has long held that the kind of skilled work that Jesus and Joseph did was carpentry.

Carpentry involves using tools to transform pieces of wood into something useful. This means that Joseph's profession, which he likely taught Jesus as a young boy, fits well into our definition of "doing technology." Jesus's first job also fulfills the call to "cultivate and keep the garden" from Genesis, meaning that Jesus was serving as a second Adam not only in his righteousness but also in his deeply human work of making. Jesus was not an abstract or idealized human but a real man in time and space, within a specific culture, doing real work with his hands and with the tools and skills his earthly father passed down to him.

When the Greek *tektōn* is translated to Latin, it becomes *faber*. Some anthropologists believe that *homo faber* ("skilled man" or "making man") is the best way to describe humans because our creation of and dependence upon tools is what sets us apart evolutionarily from other animals. Ironically, then, by the standard of the secular discipline of anthropology, the kind of work that Jesus did could not be more fundamentally human. Although Jesus would later be known by the title of "Rabbi," the title *tektōn* powerfully affirms the fullness of his human nature. And in a wonderful twist, God the Father orchestrated the story so that the day job of his Son would encompass the very thing—technology—that we sometimes mistake for hope.

Of course, the significance of Jesus's work on earth was not carpentry but what he did through the cross. And yet technology had a part to play in the center of the redemptive story as well. In another strange irony, the technology with which Jesus worked—wood and nails—was the technology on which he died—a cross.

Jesus could have been executed using any number of more "natural" means, but in the mystery of God's great plan, the way he died was decidedly technological. Under Jewish law, Jesus could have been stoned to death (see John 8:59)—which would have employed naturally occurring rocks rather than a human-made cross. Likewise, he could have been drowned, poisoned, strangled, thrown from a cliff (see Luke 4:29), or handed over to lions, any of which would have been less tool-oriented than crucifixion, one of "making man's" most horrific creations.

The Gospel of John begins by telling us that the entire world and everything in it was created by the Son of God. In Jesus's birth, God had again become immediate, walking among his creations. But then John tells us that Jesus "came to that which was his own, but his own did not receive him" (1:11). In other words, the creation turned on the Creator. This rejection reached its culmination in the cross, when God's highest creation used the creative powers he gave them to construct a tool designed to put their Creator to death. In the cross, we find the Son of God rejected by the humans he created alongside his heavenly Father, and the Son of Man murdered by the tools he used alongside his earthly father. At Golgotha, Jesus hung naked and bloody from a tree that he had spoken into existence but that humanity had transformed into a tool of death. The cross, then, is a symbol of the distorted creation turning on its Creator, a humanity transformed by sin and bent toward death.

Why, then, do we wear these grotesque distortions of sin around our necks? Why are they on top of our churches and in the background of our PowerPoint slides?

It is because Christ's transformative power goes beyond wood and nails. He has declared that the cross is no longer a symbol of deformation but of the transformative work Christ accomplished for us. Whenever we attempt to transform the natural world for destructive purposes, the cross says that God can transform that evil and restore what was lost.

After he died, Joseph of Arimathea placed Jesus's body in a tomb that someone had carved out of the ground. In addition to serving as the practical place to put a dead body, tombs function as a cultural symbol of the finality of death. Yet when the resurrected Jesus emerged from the tomb having triumphed over sin and death, he transformed the tomb into a symbol that now serves the opposite of its usual meaning.[2] In his death and resurrection, Jesus transformed the cross and the grave from symbols of death to symbols of life and the transformation that his Spirit begins to work when we believe that he is the Christ, the Son of God.

When we move out of the Gospels into the book of Revelation, we find that God has promised to continue transforming human creations meant for evil into things meant for good.

Technology and the Birth of the Church

The book of Acts begins with Jesus ascending into heaven and sending his Spirit to supernaturally empower the birth of the church. It also appears that God timed the arrival of the church to coincide with several technological developments that would aid its mission. In the centuries leading up to Jesus's birth, three major technologies had spread across the Greco-Roman world, enabling the gospel to spread like a virus on the internet.

The first was the mass use of the Greek language. When Alexander the

Great conquered most of the known world, everyone in his kingdom had to learn at least a broken form of Greek. This meant that for the first time since Babel, there was a common language among many of the peoples of the earth. But unlike Babel, where humanity tried to use a common language to show their might against God, God employed that common language as the means of transmitting the gospel to Judea, Samaria, and the ends of the earth.

For Paul and company to get to the ends of the earth, they needed a second technology—roads. In the centuries after Alexander's conquest, the Romans built roads between every major city, enabling those first missionaries to take the good news just about anywhere, extending all the way into England. Travel by sea also played a role in the spread of the church, with Paul taking several ships around the Mediterranean. Church tradition also holds that Thomas (the doubter) was able to take the gospel as far as India using the then modern transportation technology.

The final noteworthy technology is the codex, the early form of the book. In Jesus's day, anything important like Scripture was written in a scroll. There is even a scene of Jesus "unrolling" the book of Isaiah (Luke 4:17–20). But in the years before Jesus, entrepreneurial individuals began experimenting with sewing pages together into what we now call a codex. Interestingly, the early church appears to have immediately begun adopting this technology, because we have never found a scroll of any early New Testament documents. One theory is that they chose to embrace codices because they were easier to travel with. Another idea is that during the second century, some false gospels like the Gospel of Peter began to appear, and the church needed to collect the four inspired Gospels in one place. Because a scroll could not hold Matthew, Mark, Luke, and John, they used a codex to put all the canonical writings in a single volume. Although we don't know the exact reason why, we can see that God allowed the fledgling church to faithfully embrace technology as part of their mission.

A New City for a New Earth

The early church may have used some ancient technology, but what is technology's role in the future when Christ returns? Amazingly, we will see that even once God has made all things right and wiped away every tear, he does not eliminate technology. Instead he redeems even humanity's worst departures from God and his love.

Back in Genesis 4, we saw Cain build the first city in an attempt to establish an anti-garden, a place where he could distract himself from his fallenness and live apart from God. Throughout the remainder of the Scriptures, cities are often discussed in the context of curses and evil—with two notable exceptions. When God created the nation of Israel, he began to hint that he would not only restore humanity, but he would also restore many of the creations of humanity, including the city. This begins with God commanding the Israelites to designate six of their cities as places of refuge for foreigners (Num. 35:15). God was asking his people to use cities in a way that was contrary to their built-in tendencies of use and their sinful inclinations. Instead of using them to keep foreigners out, the Israelites were to use them to invite people in, into life with God and his people.

God also chose the city of Jerusalem as the place where he would dwell with his people, first in the tabernacle and later in the temple of Solomon. But even the presence of God in Zion could not make a people broken and twisted by sin follow the Law and live holy lives. Even God's handcrafted cultural goods and practices in his chosen city could not save his people. From Solomon onward, the Israelite kings worshiped idols, and the Old Testament prophets repeatedly tell of God's wrath against their sin and the sin of the people. Here is Micah's judgment against them: "Because of you Zion will be plowed like a field, Jerusalem will become a heap of rubble, and the temple hill overgrown with thickets" (Mic. 3:12).

And yet in his grace, God has still chosen the most fallen and rebellious of human creations as the place for his final restoration. God made a promise to the people of Jerusalem to restore their city, not because it was a good or worthy city but as a symbol of God's redemptive work, in which he transforms unworthy things into holy things. The very next verse in Micah portrays the restoration of Jerusalem, with God again dwelling among his creations as he did in the garden. Micah says that "many nations" and "peoples" will flow into the "Lord's temple" and that "he will teach us his ways so that we may walk in his paths" (Mic. 4:1–2). Micah's vision of the future also involves people transforming their technologies of destruction into those of cultivation: "They will beat their swords into plowshares, and their spears into pruning hooks. Nation will not lift up sword against nation, nor shall they train for war anymore" (Mic. 4:3; see also Isa. 2:4). Today, this passage might say, "They will transform their guns into garden hoses, and their tanks into tractors. Nation will not send drones against nation, nor will the people engage in social media war anymore." Micah shows us that God does not want to destroy our tools but to redeem them and transform them for human flourishing. The Old Testament visions of the future tell of the removal of sin and the dwelling of God among his people, and the place of this restoration is always the city.

Then at the end of the biblical story, when God takes the final step in his plan of redemption by restoring all things, the restoration of the city reaches its culmination. When John's Revelation tells of God creating the new heavens and new earth for the resurrected and redeemed human race (Rev. 21:1), it makes no mention of God re-creating the garden of Eden. Instead of a garden, John tells us that God will bring down from heaven a redeemed and restored city. John spends nearly the entire chapter describing all the natural materials God will use for this transformation, as he fills his city with human creations like buildings, roads, and trumpets. The theme of gold runs through the story, connecting the gold we found by the rivers of Eden (Gen. 2:12), the gold-covered, cube-shaped Holy of Holies (Ex. 25:10–16), and now the golden cube-shaped city in John's vision, described as being over 1,400 miles in length, width, and height (Rev. 21:15–16). This is meant to show that the city is so large that it would cover the entire known world at that time, radiating outward from Israel. Ellul concludes his study of the city in the Scriptures with these words: "Thus the history of the city, divided in two by Jesus Christ, goes from Eden to Jerusalem, from a garden to a city."[3]

The promise of this new city tells us that God's plan is not merely to regenerate human bodies and resurrect human souls but also to restore human creations to a world untainted by sin. Our souls are stained with sin, our bodies are destined for death, and our creations cause as many problems as they solve, but God has promised to restore them all. In the new city there will be no more sadness, pain, or death, only everlasting joy and glory to God. And although the Bible doesn't make this explicit, we can assume that some human creations—including tools and technology—will also be restored such that they too are free from evil and the unintended consequences that come with them today. N. T. Wright puts it this way:

> We will become more human, not less. If, in the present, we have been given tasks to do, vocations to pursue, the ability to delight in music and love and light and laughter, then it would be strange if, in the new creation, none of this mattered anymore.[4]

When God removes from us the ability to sin, we will no longer use our work and technology for rebellion against him. But we can also be hopeful that God will remove the problems we cause with our tools as well. What this looks like is beyond our imagination or speculation. Revelation even hints that some technology, like artificial light, will be rendered obsolete merely by the presence of the Son of God in our midst: "The city does not need the sun or the moon to shine on it, for the glory of God gives it light, and the Lamb is its lamp" (Rev. 21:23).

The presence of Emmanuel, whose name means "God with us," among his people is our greatest hope. Jesus is called the "mediator between God and mankind" (1 Tim. 2:5), and the physical presence of his resurrected person among us communicates the message that God loves us and wants to be with us. And even as we commune with the living God, the Scriptures indicate an ongoing place for technology. In fact, after Jesus rose from the dead, he gave us an enduring portrait of how we might use tools in a restored earth.

The Day God Made Breakfast

In the epilogue of his Gospel, John tells of an encounter between the resurrected Jesus and his apostles. Jesus had already appeared to Mary and the disciples twice, revealing that he had been resurrected from the dead and encouraging them to continue in faith.

Then in John 21, we find the story of Peter's restoration. After Jesus repeated his miracle of helping the disciples catch a boatload of fish, John writes, "When they landed, they saw a fire of burning coals there with fish on it, and some bread" (John 21:9). It is rather striking that Jesus, in his resurrected and glorified body, would take the time to prepare a fire and make breakfast for the disciples.

In preparing this breakfast, Jesus used simple tools to create a space for an embodied encounter between himself and Peter, and then he used that space to restore Peter to his appointed place as the leader of the disciples. Remember that the last time John told us about "a charcoal fire" was in John 18:18 (NASB), when Peter denied Jesus before the men warming themselves by the fire in the high priest's courtyard. Therefore, the fire in our current breakfast scene takes on new significance for Peter (and the Gospel reader) as Jesus transforms the meaning of fire from the place where Peter sinned to the place where Peter was restored.

Notice that the glorified Jesus didn't use an awe-inspiring miracle like a burning bush to approach Peter; rather, he simply used one of the tools of the day—charcoal—to make a meal of fish and bread. Again we see Jesus playing the role of a transformer, taking the tool of Peter's rebellion and transforming it into a tool for restoration.

We who live in the period between the garden and the city should notice that the Son of God was using tools even after his resurrection. He isn't using tools to solve a problem but, rather, to create the context for deep, full, complete human connection and presence. The Son of God "tabernacled" among us in order to bring the kingdom of God near, and here with Peter he is again performing an act of "making" by creating a place for physical nearness and spiritual restoration.

After John writes of the city coming down from heaven, he says, "I heard a loud voice from the throne, saying, 'Behold, the *tabernacle* of God is among the people, and He will dwell among them, and they shall be His people, and God Himself will be among them'" (Rev. 21:3 NASB, emphasis mine).

Until that day, the New Testament urges us to continue using physical tools—specifically the Table and the Cup—to create a space for the embodied fellowship of believers. Paul writes, "Whenever you eat this bread and drink this cup, you proclaim the Lord's death until he comes" (1 Cor. 11:26). Fascinatingly, God did not choose for us to use grain and grapes to celebrate and experience his Son's work, but bread and wine, a product of human creativity. In a world that values speed and efficiency, the slow act of making and sharing bread together powerfully expresses the value, meaning, and identity as the people of God.

Throughout the Epistles, Paul, Peter, and John express their deep desire to be physically present with those to whom they wrote.[5] Often, the apostle writers connect "joy" and "fullness" to being physically present, and they report sadness and longing when they cannot see their friends. And yet, as we see in John's Epistles (2 John 12; 3 John 13–14), they still used communication tools when face-to-face encounters were not possible and when the use of those tools could build up the body of Christ in other ways. However, their intention was to honor the incarnation of Christ by encouraging physical nearness and attentive presence whenever possible.

These two eschatological images from John—of our resurrected Lord cooking breakfast and of the glorified Lord bringing down a restored city—tell us that our hope resides in the presence of God among his people. But they also tell us that we shouldn't view technology as a temporary aberration of the fallen world. Instead, Jesus has offered a portrait of technology according to God's original design, for his glory and for the building up of the body of Christ through embodied life. Our tools are still flawed and problematic, but we have the promise that God will somehow restore even them to a sinless state, from our sinful uses and the trade-offs and downsides they often bring.

Dealing with Unintended Consequences

Until Christ's return, we are faced with the challenge of how to faithfully embrace technology in our own time. We know we should avoid using technology for evil and selfish gain. But even when we create technologies that we think of as deeply redemptive and restorative, they can sometimes create unintended side effects. For example, cochlear implants that restore hearing to the deaf would seem to offer a portrait of the restoration that God will one day bring. But in deaf families who have developed a culture around sign language and other practices, a cochlear implant can send an unintended message that the person using it doesn't want to be a part of that culture.

Trade-offs and unintended consequences come in most design processes, even in something as benign as a soccer ball. For example, during one World Cup, Adidas introduced the Fevernova ball, designed to make the ball follow a more consistent and predicable flight pattern than the previous generation of balls. However, many players complained that it was too light, making it fly unpredictably. For the next World Cup, Adidas attempted to fix those problems with the +Teamgeist ball. The new curved panels that were bonded together were supposed to make it uniformly round and completely waterproof, but this time players felt that the ball flew too fast and made it too easy to score goals. The next ball was called the Jabulani, and it had textured grooves to give the ball the same kind of aerodynamics as a traditional stitched ball. Again, some players complained that the new grooves made the ball fly unpredictably.

The point of this illustration is to expose something we don't always like to admit—that every good technology comes with a trade-off of some kind. Newer tools bring benefits, but those benefits come with a cost. Even the VP of Product at Facebook, Chris Cox, admitted as much when he said, "Facebook solved this problem of getting all your friends in one place, and created the problem of having all your friends in one place."[6] Even when inventors have the best of intentions for their creations, not everyone is able to benefit equally. As Neil Postman said, "The advantages and disadvantages of new technologies are never distributed evenly among the population. This means that every new technology benefits some and harms others."[7]

As creators, we have a responsibility to attempt to mitigate these risks and build technology in an ethical way that includes a process for thinking about secondary effects. And, as end users, we need to be regularly evaluating out technology usage in community to see how it is affecting us and whether we are living faithfully with it.

A Theological Technology Tetrad

To help us think about how we use technology and how it uses us, I have created a simple chart with four boxes. We know there are good and bad *uses* of technology, but that we also need to be attentive to the unintentional *effects* of technology (i.e., why technology is not neutral). Let's start by considering something simple, a shovel, thinking through its uses and effects, both positive and negative. There are good uses of the shovel, like building a church or garden, and bad uses, like hurting someone or burying stolen goods. But as we've said, it's also important to think through the unintentional effects that happen irrespective of morality, like blisters and bigger muscles. Here it is in chart form:

Shovel	Positive	Negative
Intentional	Building a church or garden	Stealing and burying treasure
Unintentional	Stronger muscles	Blisters and calluses

This can be a helpful way of understanding any technology, including digital technology like phones and social media or online church and online education. Each of these is worthy of careful, nuanced discussion, but we'll start with social media as an example to stimulate deeper thinking in your own community. Social media allows many wonderful ways to share life's joys with one another, and of course there are also evil ways to use it, including bullying, bragging, and rage. Those negative uses tend to receive most of our focus and critique, but we also want to think carefully about how our minds and bodies adapt to technology the longer we use it. On the positive side, sometimes we find ourselves exposed to new ideas and people that can enrich and deepen our thinking and faith. And yet, some of the patterns built into social media (speed, likes, etc.) can shape us in a direction that seeks unhealthy levels of attention and can distract us from things we want to spend more time on.

Social Media	Positive	Negative
Intentional	Encouraging friends, being informed, celebrating events	Bullying, bragging, rage, racism, sexism
Unintentional	Exposure to different people and ideas	Distraction, attention span, self-focus

We can also extend this grid to more complex technologies like genetically modified plants, which is an extension of the ways humans have modified plants through breeding for generations. Again, this example will be oversimplified, but we can generically say that it is positive to create food that can feed more people as global temperatures change. At the same time, genetic modification of food can also be used to create unhealthy power structures that favor profit-driven companies over local, community farmers. But even in the best case, when scientists work hard to breed and modify an organism designed for human flourishing, there can be unintentional negative side effects such as the new plant affecting another local organism, which upsets the larger ecosystem. Still, there are hopeful examples where a GMO plant can reduce the number of pesticides needed while still protecting older varieties.

GMOs	Positive	Negative
Intentional	Heat-tolerant plants that feed more people	Controlling and limiting food supplies
Unintentional	Protecting non-GMOs, reducing pesticides	New variety that affects local insects and honey

Technology and the Story of God

We can tie this back into the biblical story by noticing that these four categories of technology roughly correspond to the four chapters of the biblical story as we've been telling it. Our intentionally good uses of technology are often *redemptive*, while the unintentionally good things that sometimes come with a new tool can be a *reflection* of the mystery of God's image. On the one side, the intentionally evil things we do with technology are part of our *rebellion* against God, and the unintentional side effects that come with technology make us long for *restoration*.

This allows us to update our chart with the theological categories that can add additional depth to the way we think about the tools we use:

	Positive	Negative
Intentional	3. Redemption	2. Rebellion
Unintentional	1. Reflection	4. Restoration

Retelling the story in order, we started with creation, where we found that our ability to make technology is a *reflection* of our Creator (number 1 in the chart). Among the things we create, technology is the "human activity of using tools to transform God's creation for practical purposes." Our phones, for example, reflect God's nature as relational and communicative, and they transform our relationships and the physical space of the world.

Second, from the fall, we found that every technology has the potential to be used for sin and *rebellion*. Embedded in every tool is a tendency of usage from which a set of values emerge. Our flesh will often seize upon the power and value system of a tool and use it for evil. And humans have certainly found all kinds of ways to employ technology like phones in service of selfish gain and destruction.

But even though tools can be used for rebellion, we also found that technology can be used for *redemptive* purposes (number 3), temporarily overcoming the effects of the fall and serving the embodied life of Christ in the believer. Phones can reconnect those who cannot be physically present together, and they can be used to coordinate and enrich the time when we can be present. However, we also found that all mediums communicate meaning, that they create new cultures, and shape thinking. Sometimes, for all the good they offer, our technology also brings with it a series of trade-offs and unintended consequences.

Thankfully, at the end of the biblical story, we find that God's plans include the *restoration* of all things (number 4), including some of the things we make. Normally we think of *restoration* in purely positive terms, but here we can think of restoration in terms of highlighting the problems of technology today that God will solve then. When possible, we should work toward reforming technology in light of the new heavens and new earth, attempting to reduce trade-offs wherever we can while also acknowledging that some problems will never be relieved until the new city arrives.

The category of restoration is not meant to be an excuse in regard to the problems of technology. On the contrary, carefully considering the trade-offs and problems of technology should urge us to create and use tools that fit within God's command to both "cultivate" and "keep" the garden. And if we are not in the position of creating such tools, we need to spend time considering the value systems that emerge from using a tool; we must discern when those tools are in conflict with the value system of the kingdom of God. Just as the promise of our future resurrection does not imply that we are free to neglect our souls and bodies, the promise of restoration does not give us license to create or use tools that abuse God's creation and distort the kind of life he has commanded us to live.

Thinking about technology through this tetrad of questions also gives us an opportunity to worship God whenever we use tools. When something works well, it is reflecting the order and creativity of God. Rather than praising Apple, we can praise the God who created Steve Jobs in his image. When something enables us to further God's kingdom and restore something that was lost in the fall, we again have the chance to praise God for graciously allowing us to create even in our sinful state. But we must also be ardent in our insistence that the redemptive capacities of technology are limited and temporary. We cannot mistake their power for the power of the One who one day will finally redeem us. Instead, let us view the redemptive functions of our tools as a foreshadowing of what is to come.

At the same time, when we see unspeakable evil conducted with and through technology, it is not cause for us to hate or fear technology but for us to hate the sin that shackles us all. Medical technology can give us a glimpse and foretaste of the coming world when all things will be healed. But one day the medicine will no longer save us from physical death, so let us redirect our hope away from our tools and to the One who will restore the full range of our humanity—human souls, human bodies, and human creations.

In the next two chapters, we will pick up the history of technology where the Bible leaves off and explore two major technological periods, both of which can be understood as an alternative story to the way the Bible looks at technology. First we'll see how this holds up in the digital age as we shift from physical tools to modern electronic devices. Then we'll return to the idea of technology and imagination and see how an alternate story of the place of technology has emerged.

QUESTIONS

- Fill out the chart below for a technology you use, are creating, or are still evaluating:

	Positive	Negative
Intentional		
Unintentional		

- What technologies do you think will be in the new heaven and new earth? What technology *won't* be there?
- How can you use your technology today in light of the day when God will make all things new and right and beautiful?

10

TECHNICISM

"The future is going to be awesome!"

When you read that sentence, does it sound more like a statement of theological hope or technological hope? Is it expressing a profound trust that Christ will return to make all things new, or is it another headline about some tech that's just around the corner, promising to change our lives for the better?

As we found in the opening chapters of this book, technology, imagination, and ideas about the future are deeply intertwined. We create stories to imagine how the world could be, and we create technology to change the world into what we imagine. Both activities are oriented toward the future, looking from how the world is now toward how it could be one day. Our Christian faith too can be understood as a story that points to a promise about the future. God made us to be cocreators and gave us the gift of technology as part of our role to have dominion over the earth and fill the universe with new wonders. Sadly, we allowed the virus of sin to enter the system, corrupting us and the things we make. But God's story is not done yet.

He is working to restore all things, and in the meantime, we can continue to use technology to fulfill our creative calling now and offer foretastes of the healing he has promised in the future.

However, as human technology becomes increasingly powerful, it is sometimes difficult to distinguish between technological and theological hope. Religious people praise technology, while technologists sometimes speak in religious terms. In his book *The Religion of Technology*, David Noble writes,

> While religious leaders promote their revival of spirit through an avid and accomplished use of the latest technological advances, scientists and technologists increasingly attest publicly to the value of their work in the pursuit of divine knowledge.[1]

This has allowed a subtle counterstory to emerge that hits many of the same beats as the biblical movement but that offers a different savior and a different goal. Historically, these two stories have an interwoven development, with each informing the other but also disagreeing and eventually diverging. In this chapter, we will look at how the promise of technological salvation emerged in both explicit forms and in subtle everyday realities, and then we will offer a counter set of practices that grounds technology in its proper place in the movement of God.

Has Technology Made the World a Better Place?

Looking over the twentieth and twenty-first centuries, there has been tremendous technological innovation for good and for ill. The two world wars and the global wars that followed it were increasingly violent due to increasingly destructive technology, from tanks to nuclear weapons to drones. At the same time, advances in medicine, food, and education have brought tremendous changes around the world in terms of human flourishing and dignity. According to ourworldindata.org, from 1820 to 2020 the percentage of people living in poverty dropped from over 90 percent to under 10 percent. Over this same period, the number of children who died before reaching age five has dropped from over 40 percent to less than 5 percent, literacy rates have grown from 12 percent to 85 percent, and the number of people living in a democracy with some level of freedom has increased from less than 5 percent to more than 50 percent. These trends are cause for celebration because it means that more humans are able to take part in the kind of thriving, image-bearing life God originally intended. This allows us to say that, for all its downsides, technology has brought about some positive trends.

And yet, these positive trends sometimes lead us to put faith in the promise of technology to solve deeper issues. Kevin Kelly, in his book *What Technology Wants*, lists several tools whose creators promised that their devices would bring world peace.[2] For example, Hiram Maxim, the inventor of the machine gun, insisted his invention would "make war impossible." Alfred Nobel believed his invention, dynamite, would "sooner lead to peace than a thousand world conventions." When Nobel realized that his tool was bringing about the exact opposite, he founded the Nobel Prize in hopes that his legacy would be one of peace instead of destruction. But it wasn't just weapon makers who thought their tools could prevent war; Orville Wright believed that the airplane he and his brother invented would "have a tendency to make war impossible." Guglielmo Marconi believed his radio and "the coming wireless era" would "make war impossible." In the early 2000s, there was hope that the "One Laptop Per Child" initiative[3] would bring peace to wartorn regions of the world, but it appears not to have had this effect.

In a sense, this promise that technology can solve our deepest problems goes all the way back to humanity's first days outside the garden of Eden. While the people of God place their hope in God's promise to restore his creation, wipe away our sins, resurrect our bodies, and bring down a glorious new city from heaven, the enemies of God tell an alternate story. Beginning with Cain, the alternative vision says that humans will find their salvation in the city and its technology. The city presents us a welcome distraction from our sin, and its power creates the illusion that we can live apart from God. One day, we tell ourselves, the technology of the city will become our savior, rescuing us even from death. As St. Augustine wrote long ago,

[The] two cities have been formed out of two loves: the earthly [city] by the love of the self, even to the contempt of God; the heavenly [city] by the love of God, even to the contempt of self. The former, in a word, glories in itself, the latter in the Lord. For the one seeks glory from men; but the greatest glory of the other is God.[4]

Today we can see these two divergent views of technology in the way our culture conceives of progress. As modern people, part of our myth is that technology is always progressing, and that any problems caused by technology can be solved by applying more technology to the technological problems. Of course, technology often does solve problems, and later generations of technology tend to have fewer problems than the first generation. However, over time our culture has begun to believe that technology will one day solve *all* of our problems, leading to a kind of utopia.

The Counterstory Emerges

Stephen Monsma calls the idea that technology will solve all our problems "technicism."[5] He argues that over time technicism has become a kind of unspoken religion for the secular world. For those who don't see God as an anchoring point for reality, technological progress has become a new story that offers means of salvation and a source of future hope.

Early Christian writers did not often consider the role of technology in their lives, but this slowly shifted over time. For example, during the fourth century, Benedictine monks began to emphasize the practical arts for the way they enhanced their commitment to manual labor. John Scotus Erigena (815–877) was one of the first thinkers to argue that the "image of God" should not be considered a purely spiritual concept but should extend to our physical bodies and acts of making. Later, as we learned in chapter 4, Hugh of St. Victor (1096–1141) elevated technology and carpentry as a "mechanical philosophy" alongside theology, math, and economics.

These are indications that in the first thousand years of the Western, Christian world, there was an increasing value placed on technology and the creative abilities God had given humanity. In the centuries between about

1200 and 1600, this acceptance of technology began to accelerate with a flurry of intellectual, scientific, and technological development throughout Europe. During the Renaissance, major works of art such as Michelangelo's Sistine Chapel and sculpture of David were created. Then in the scientific revolution, thinkers like Copernicus, Kepler, Newton, and even Galileo made major discoveries about the laws of physics and how the universe works. At the same time, men like Leonardo da Vinci began experimenting with ever more complex and powerful tools, drawing up plans for everything from helicopters to firearms. Accurate timekeeping tools were also invented during this period, as well as ships with ranges long enough to explore the "New World."

Over time, as these developments stacked up, people began to think of these new tools in terms of "mastery over nature." For the first time, philosophers started to speak of progress not in moral or civil terms but in relationship to advances in technology. These technological innovations gave humanity more and more control over the natural world, and people began to hope technology would one day remove all human suffering from the planet. Many of these thinkers were Christians such as Francis Bacon, who wrote,

> For man by the fall fell at the same time from his state of innocence and from his dominion over creation. Both of these losses, however, can even in this life be in some part repaired; the former by religion and faith, the latter by arts and sciences.[6]

But notice that Bacon sees two separate problems with two separate solutions. The first problem is the stain of sin that Bacon believes God alone can repair. As for the second problem—dominion over creation—Bacon thinks technology (i.e., "arts and sciences") can do some good. However, he is guarded in his hope about technology, saying it can solve problems only "in some part." But over time, many thinkers rejected this limited expectation of technology and began to see science and technology as a means of freeing humanity from their need for God, from sin, and even from mortality.

Somewhere around 1650, in the middle of this scientific and technological progress, there was a major shift in the way people conceived of the
world. The period before 1650 is often called the "premodern" period, and
after 1650 is referred to as the "modern" period. In the premodern period,
almost everyone was religious in the sense of believing in a God or gods who
set in place the fixed moral rules of the world. In fact, just about everything
in life was fixed: where people lived, their jobs, the location of the nearby
river or distant mountain—these were all preordained givens, like the laws
of the universe given by the gods.

But the technological advances in the centuries leading up to the 1600s
(and even more inventions that would soon follow) meant that people no
longer had to see the world as a set of immobile objects. Rivers could now
be redirected, and mountains could now be moved. But moving a mountain no longer required faith the size of a mustard seed, only sufficiently
advanced technology and science.

The philosophers of the day started to write that if the objects in the world
weren't fixed, then maybe the moral and religious laws of the universe weren't
either. And if there are no absolute moral laws, then there is no problem of
innocence to overcome. The generations after Bacon argued that "spiritual"
problems were the creation of imaginary religions, and science proved that our
problems were physical obstacles that technology could eventually overcome.

At the time, most Europeans were Christians who believed that future
hope belonged to Christ's return, when he will make all things right. When
they looked at a timeline of history, they saw the return of Christ at the end.
But in the shift from premodernity to modernity, Jesus was kicked off the
end of the timeline and replaced with technology. In previous eras, athe-
ism had never been a truly viable belief system, and it attracted few people.
But as science and technology continued to progress, the need for God
appeared to grow dimmer and dimmer. The power of technology was one
of the factors that led Friedrich Nietzsche to make his famous declaration
that "God is dead."[7] Of course, Nietzsche didn't mean that God had literally died—he meant that the story we've been telling ourselves about a God
who runs the universe no longer made any sense in a world where humans

could control the natural world with technology. Nietzsche believed that humanity needed a new story to replace the one about God. It turns out that technology offered the perfect replacement.

If we put all the elements together, we can see that technicism has all the elements of a good religion, offering parallels to the Christian story. In the following chart we can see how the story begins, what problem needs to be solved, what event we are waiting for, and the goal of existence.

Origin	Problem	Solution	Timing	Goal
Divine	Sin	Jesus	His Return	Resurrection
Chance	Physicality	Technology	Singularity	Transcendence

Instead of viewing humanity as uniquely created in the image of God with a purpose and a destiny, the alternate story sees humanity as simply the next stage of what emerges by chance.[8] Instead of acknowledging that the root of the difficulties in life is sin, a spiritual reality that has physical consequences, the alternate story sees our image-bearing human bodies as the ultimate problem to be solved. Futurist Ray Kurzweil writes, "I regard the freeing of the human mind from its severe physical limitations of scope and duration as the necessary next step in evolution. Evolution, in my view, represents the purpose of life. That is, the purpose of life—and of our lives—is to evolve."[9] Kurzweil goes on to write that the advancement of technology is a kind of spiritual ascension where humankind is moving ever upward, eventually leading to a place where we free ourselves from the physical world and live in a heavenlike state. Although not everyone is as explicit as Kurzweil,[10] he serves as an example of how religious language can be repurposed for a religion of technology that sees technology as a savior. To get to technicism's goal, a few other technologies are needed, including major advances in artificial intelligence.

Artificial Intelligence

If humans are ever to truly escape our bodies, we need exponentially more advanced technology than we currently have. But humans won't create this technology—technology will create this technology. In the thinking of technicism, there is a coming event that functions like a religious future hope (or eschatology) called the "singularity," which is the moment when our computers become smarter than all of humanity put together, giving them the ability to invent tools that our tiny little minds can't even imagine. This is based on the hope that AI will continue to progress to the point where it is more and more humanlike in its abilities, eventually outstripping our collective intelligence and inventing the tools we need in order to transcend.

Discussions of AI sometimes see a progression from Artificial Narrow Intelligence (ANI), meaning machines that are good at one thing (like we have now), to Artificial General Intelligence (AGI), machines that are as good as humans at many things (your average sci-fi robot), to Artificial Super Intelligence (ASI), where machines are much better than humans at everything (and hopefully remain benevolent). Today's ANIs are better than humans at many tasks such as flying planes, diagnosing illnesses, and offering fair prison sentences. At the same time, their limitations mean they sometimes make mistakes that humans wouldn't always make or pick up human biases. Whether we realize it or not, AI is already everywhere, making decisions in your antilock brakes, ensuring your photos are lit well, learning your anxieties and vanities for advertisers, and identifying your voice as you turn out the lights.

For all the good AI does for us, we should not be surprised that some are using AI in openly evil ways that violate privacy, steal secrets, and incite or enable violence. Beyond humans using AI for evil intent, even many tech entrepreneurs express caution around the potential unintended consequences of AI, worrying that if we give too much power to AIs they could make catastrophic mistakes. In the classic "paper clip scenario," an AI is given a task to maximize efficiency of paper clip production, but it accidentally destroys the earth by converting everything into paper clips.[11] This is an unlikely and outlandish scenario, but it is used to illustrate the problems in moving beyond Artificial Narrow Intelligence. It is difficult to know if AI will ever reach general or special intelligence, but achieving this may lead to unprecedented change. In the meantime, Christians cannot afford to operate out of a posture of fear (see Josh. 10:1) but rather must be involved in the development of AI itself and the legal and ethical frameworks that put guardrails around AI and our use of it. As with all technology, AI offers as many opportunities for redemptive change as it does for exploitation, but beyond these good and bad uses, we also must be aware of the more subtle ways AI influences our thinking and expectations of the good life.[12] For example, pastor-theologian Joshua Smith has been exploring the topic of robot personhood, both because this will be important sooner than we realize, but also because it relates to how we understand the dignity of human persons, theologically and in the legal system.[13] This is just one of many examples of why AI may be the source of the most challenging theological and ethical questions of this century.

Related to the promise of the coming singularity, technicism also has a concept of salvation and eternal life, which will occur when the post singularity computers invent tools that enable all humans to live forever, ushering in the posthuman era.

The Posthuman Promise

Transhumanism and posthumanism are related but slightly different concepts. Transhumanism is a philosophical idea focused on using technology to enhance the human condition by extending human life and increasing our physical and cognitive abilities. At face value, this is not directly in conflict with a Christian conception of the role of technology, and there is even a Christian Transhumanist Society that seeks dialogue on these matters with atheists and those of other faiths. Posthumanism moves beyond transhumanism to the belief that with enough technological enhancements, humans will eventually evolve beyond our current limitations, enabling us to become powerful beings who live forever and achieve transcendence. Understood this way, transhumanism is the method, while posthumanism is a goal.[14] Transhumanist technology ranges from medicines that prevent cancer and prolong life, to replacement limbs that make a person faster or stronger, to gadgets that could increase mental capacity, and even to "virtue enhancement," which would prevent humans from doing things like lying. It also includes various gene editing technologies that could pass such attributes on to one's children.

Here we should make a key distinction between technology that is *restorative* (wearing glasses that restore poor eyesight, replacing a limb lost in an accident) and technology that *enhances* a human beyond our natural abilities. The transhumanist goal of improving the human condition is a worthy one, and there are many restorative technologies we should support and use. But at some point, technologies that seek to enhance humanity move into theologically and ethically murky territory. While there may be some gray areas, I think it's fair to say that the posthumanist goal of fundamentally altering humanity until we are a new species takes us outside of God's intentions for human nature and technology. And yet, as we saw in the beginning of the chapter, technology has made many aspects of human life better and reduced human suffering, so there are opportunities for Christians to work alongside transhumanists and other technologists in the pursuit of human flourishing. We should avoid the explicit rejection of the resurrection offered by Christ as the ultimate hope of humanity, but we can find ways to embrace those technologies that align with the values of God's kingdom while working to offset their unintended effects.

Most of the time, faith in technology doesn't look this explicitly religious. If you ask the average person if technology is the "savior of humanity," he or she probably wouldn't embrace that kind of language. And even if we say there is a religion of technology in Silicon Valley, the average Google or Tesla worker wouldn't openly claim it as their belief system. Instead, the characteristics of technicism take more subtle forms, three of which we'll explore below. These include the tendency to elevate the value of machines over the value of humans (first seen in the Luddite controversy), the belief in marketing about what we need to be happy, and ever shifting standards for the good life.

Luddites: Machine Over Man

Often the word "Luddite" is used for someone who is antitechnology, but the real story behind this term demonstrates a key turning point in the valuing of technology over human life. During the Industrial Revolution, many new machines were invented that could perform tasks more efficiently than individual workers. This new manufacturing equipment allowed business owners to increase their profits because they could replace ten laborers with a single person who pushed a button on a machine. The problem was that the other nine men lost their jobs.

With no way to earn money for their families, many fell into poverty and despair. According to legend, in 1779 a man named Ned Ludd was fed up with the takeover of the machines and took his anger out on two knitting machines. The news of Ned's rage against the machines spread quickly, and groups of masked men fed up with their livelihood being taken over by machines started breaking into factories all over England and destroying manufacturing equipment. Whenever a machine was found destroyed, people would whisper, "Ned Ludd did it."

It's easy to see how the term "Luddite" became associated with the fear of technology and technological change. But the writings the Luddites left behind indicate that their main concern was not technology itself but the fact that technological thinking had convinced business owners to value their machines more than human life. In fact, in 1721, the British government made machine destruction a capital offense. God had said, "Whoever sheds human blood, by humans shall their blood be shed, for in the image of God has God made mankind" (Gen. 9:6). But the new laws said in effect, "Whoever sheds the blood of a machine, by a machine shall their blood be shed, for mankind has made machine into a god of their own image."

While many of the Luddites were simply angry that they lost their jobs and livelihoods—and their acts of destruction were clearly wrong—it is hard to disagree with their sentiment that humankind had made the turn toward valuing machine life more than human life. In the late twentieth century this had taken on new forms, with many kinds of manual labor being replaced by robots. The changes that come with a more robotic workforce is a clear case of the trade-offs of technology. On the one hand, AIs and robots can relieve human workers of tedious, repetitive, or dangerous tasks. For example, auditors who perform the monotonous task of combing through tax returns to look for anomalies might be able to turn over their work to software that can work 24/7. But this brings up the other side of technological expansion, namely, what happens to the workers who get replaced by machines. From farmers, truck drivers, and soldiers to auditors, lawyers, and receptionists, almost no job sector will be unaffected by AI. Many reports claim that for every 10 million jobs replaced by AI, 10 million new, less tedious, more creative jobs will be created in their place. But even if all those jobs are created, this level of change will present hardships for many people during the transition.

Medicine will also be changed by AI. From diagnosis to robots that monitor and care for the elderly, technology has the potential to reduce errors and increase care while also potentially decreasing human-to-human connection.

Thankfully, destroying machines is no longer a capital offense, but we have many challenges ahead of us. Taking a few steps back in time again, we'll see that there were other forms of the antihuman, pro-technology spirit that came with the rise of consumerist capitalism and advertising in the post–Industrial Revolution society.

Marketing: Tell Me What I Need

The technological advances of the past few centuries are, as we've said, not themselves morally evil. In fact, those advances brought humanity unprecedented material wealth and prosperity. Developments in medicine, plumbing, food preparation, and so on led to a world where average Europeans and Americans had access to clean water, adequate food, and sufficient shelter (these effects would reach Asia, South America, and much of Africa in the following century). The Industrial Revolution is known for many of its negative practices like child labor and filling the air with smog, but these new factories were able to efficiently produce basic goods at a low enough cost that even people with very little income could afford them. The standard of living in the industrialized world continued to grow steadily in the decades leading up to 1900, resulting in increased life expectancy and decreased infant mortality.

Then, around the turn of the twentieth century, things started to shift in an unforeseen direction. The factories were becoming so efficient at producing goods that they began making more goods than people previously needed. Today, the idea that a factory might produce something no one wants to buy is rather ordinary, but in the history of humanity, this had never happened before. Basic goods were always scarce, as they still are today in developing countries, but suddenly factory owners were facing a question no one had ever asked before: "What do we do with all this extra stuff?"[15]

They had two choices before them. On the one hand, they could choose to produce fewer goods, but this would mean running their machines less frequently and leaving excess capacity, driving up the cost of production and raising prices. If prices went up, then competitors who chose not to decrease production could easily outsell them at lower prices. Ironically, the advances in manufacturing technology increased to a tipping point that threatened to destroy the prosperity it had created.

The second option for business owners was to keep producing as efficiently as possible, and then work to convince customers to buy things they didn't think they needed. This continues the trend of valuing machines and products over the true needs of human beings. This meant they needed to be more aggressive in telling potential customers about the benefits of their products. Up to that point, advertisements for products mostly consisted of the name, the price, and a list of the product's features. But as we found in chapter 8, using photography and later video enabled advertisers to move customers in a way printed text and line drawings never could.

Advertising is not just about conveying information; it's about moving people to an action, sometimes convincing people to buy things they didn't think they needed. Over time, advertisers figured out that if they linked their products not just to a list of features but to emotional feelings and even transcendent ideals, people would feel more compelled to buy them. For example, all one needs to get clean enough to be safe from germs is a simple bar of soap that costs almost nothing. But most of us don't buy the cheapest soap because we've been convinced that more expensive soaps will go beyond making us clean—they will make us feel happy.

It's that "feel happy" part that advertisers had to tap into to urge people to buy things that go above basic necessities. Advertisers drew on the power of different mediums to create characters like the famous Marlboro man—a strong, loner cowboy—convincing smokers they could experience his life when they bought a pack of Marlboros. Today the company that has mastered the art of linking emotional images and transcendent wording to its products is Apple. Apple describes its products as "magical," "revolutionary," and "amazing," and features videos that almost seem to caress their latest devices. The original logo went so far as to put a happy rainbow on the symbol of sin and decay, the forbidden fruit. Today, that logo has been transformed into a brilliant, flawless white light reassuring us of its power and beauty.[16]

For advertisers, mastering language and images was only part of the problem. Two more issues were outstanding. First, advertisers needed a way to get those messages into homes. Newspapers and magazines weren't quite enough to deliver the sales volume they needed. They needed something more powerful and more pervasive. In the late 1800s, that powerful tool was created: the radio.

Radio technology was used quite effectively by the Allied and German militaries during World War I, but initially radio was too costly to have any use in the consumer market. Unlike newspapers, there was no way to charge listeners for the radio programs and therefore no way to make money from broadcasting. Yet advertisers knew that using radio to transmit commercials into homes would give them unprecedented public mind share, if only they could figure out a way to offer something other than twenty-four-hour advertisements. One particularly memorable pioneer in expanding radio for advertising was John Romulus Brinkley, a Depression-era quack doctor who claimed to have invented a cure for male impotence (which I think is best not to repeat here). Although many doctors discredited his method, he realized the potential of radio, building his own radio station in Kansas to promote his procedure, alongside other products in between popular talk shows and music. The plan worked, helping him earn over $10 million per year (in today's value) at the height of his radio empire. He eventually lost his medical license and radio license, forcing him to move to Mexico where he could continue his broadcasts across the border.[17]

Brinkley's example is extreme, but it illustrates how the programs people listened to—and later watched on television—were Trojan horses for advertisements. People loved listening to breaking news and hearing exciting stories, all paid for by advertisers whose goal was to inject into homes the message that new products and technology had the power to make their lives better. And they were terribly effective at getting this message across . . . leading to the next problem for advertisers.

Eventually, people started to believe that they needed all those excess goods the factories were pumping out. The problem was that people simply couldn't afford to buy them. Fortunately for product makers, there was an easy fix that would actually make them even more money. All they had to do was loan people the money they didn't have and convince them to pay it out over time—with interest.

The burgeoning credit market opened up more money to buy more things. Product makers continued to create new products, convincing people that buying them would bring happiness. Then they offered people more money to buy all of it. This powerful cycle continues today and, as we all know, it has started to catch up with us. The economic crisis of 2008 can be traced back to that powerful moment when people were convinced that technology can make life better and—with just a little more credit—better life can be theirs right now.

Today, marketers have even more powerful digital tools to reach customers. As we saw in chapter 8, social media platforms are funded by gathering as much information about people as possible and selling that information to other companies who combine it with other data sources that help create highly targeted ads. For example, if you visit a friend for a few days, you might later see an ad for the same kind of toothpaste they let you borrow at their house. This is not because your phone is recording your conversation about toothpaste; it is because marketers can combine data from your friend's credit card purchases, your GPS movements indicating you were at their house overnight, and the social media connection detailing your relationship. One day, advertisers will start using our voices—not just the content of our conversation but the emotional tone we convey as we speak. Scholars like Joseph Turow have explored ways that our biometric data can be used to deepen the targeting power of technology, and his most recent book title summarizes the concern quite well: *The Voice Catchers: How Marketers Listen In to Exploit Your Feelings, Your Privacy, and Your Wallet.*[18] The point is that we must be wary of what our true needs and desires are rather than succumbing to a technologically enabled version of what will make us happy.

"Better" Becomes a Moving Target

This is not to say that technology doesn't make anything better, for it certainly does that in many cases. We have access to unprecedented levels of prosperity, and we live in a world where almost anything is available at the push of a button. Only the most powerful kings of old could afford to taste the kinds of food that anyone can buy at the supermarket today, and only the most adventurous of history's sailors would ever set foot in the far-off lands that anyone with a valid passport can visit today. All accounts indicate that today's workers are in fact more productive on the whole than workers in previous generations. The US Bureau of Labor and Statistics, which has been tracking productivity since the 1960s, says that workers today are producing almost three times as much as workers sixty years ago.[19]

Yet this prosperity and productivity bring with them a shift in how we see the world and what we expect from it. To support all of this productivity and advancement, people began moving from the country into cities of ever-increasing size, and then into larger and larger homes in those cities. Families who once worked together on a farm now spent much of their day separated as Dad went off to work and Mom stayed home to care for the house. Thankfully, in the 1940s and 1950s many modern conveniences—vacuum cleaners, dishwashers, microwaves, and lawn mowers—came on the market, and many people believed these new devices would make work completely obsolete. They wondered if everyone would retire in their late thirties and sit around with nothing to do.

But this promise never materialized. Instead, people began to work more hours and have less free time. In her book *More Work for Mother*, Ruth Schartz Cowen argues that mothers actually took on *more* work during the "industrialization of the home" than ever before.[20] How did this happen? Of course there were a variety of factors at play, but one of the major factors was the shifting of expectations. Before vacuum cleaners, people had to use brooms to clean their houses. Vacuum cleaners made housecleaning go much faster, but other changes counteracted this benefit. First, people started buying larger homes, giving them more to clean. Second, they moved to suburbs far away from work and relationships. With fathers heading into the city and fewer nearby friends and family, mothers were left with a larger workload to do in isolation. Finally, with all the new cleaning products and knowledge of germs and medicine, expectations of cleanliness shifted. The result was more to clean, more often, and with stronger tools. Instead of freeing up time to be with family and friends, there grew an expectation of what a person should have and how it should look.

The shifts in expectations continue with every new technology. In my pocket is a phone that is hundreds of times more powerful than the computer I had as a kid. Yet, I regularly think of things I wish it would do better, even though it does things I never imagined a phone could do just a few years ago. Each year a new soccer ball—like the World Cup balls we discussed in the previous chapter—comes along, solving some problems and introducing new ones. Of course, the new ball is usually better, but our definition of "better" has shifted as well. This cycle of progressive improvement and altered expectations has led to what we now call consumerism and materialism. Nothing is ever good enough, and we find ourselves continually distracted from our deeper spiritual needs that no tool can solve. At the same time, although worker productivity is on the rise and the expectation of more is everywhere, actual wages have not risen proportionally since the 1980s, and the wealth gap has grown significantly, partially enabled by new technology.

Jesus tells us that we should "store up . . . treasures in heaven" not "treasures on earth" (Matt. 6:19–20), but this is challenging to do under the subtle influence of modern technology. Not only do modern tools help reinforce technicism and perpetuate consumerism, but the instant availability of today's technologies brings with it a fundamental change to human life, which most of us never even notice. To live faithfully in this world, we must resist not only the obvious evil uses of technology but also the hidden messages it sends, many of which are counter to the kingdom of God.

QUESTIONS

- Do you think technology has made the world better or worse? How does that affect your view of technology, God, and the future?
- Do you think AI will ever reach a kind of sentience that could lead to the singularity? What do you think the limits of transhumanism should be?
- What forms of technicism (valuing technology over humanity, always needing more) do you see in your everyday life and world?
- How can you avoid the negative tendencies in the culture of technicism and redirect your technology creation and usage toward human flourishing?

11

VIRTUALIZATION

FROM CREATION AND THE fall through the redemptive story of the crucifixion and into the future restoration of all things, we have seen that technology plays an important role in what it means to be one of God's image
bearers. But how are the ancient tools of the biblical story related to the
modern devices of the digital age? How can we live as faithful Christians
in an always-on, hyperconnected world? To explore these questions, I will
begin this chapter with some of my experiences as a digital creative before
moving on to reflect on what it means for our cultural goods to be virtual-
ized, especially considering new frontiers in technology. In the latter half of
the chapter, we will consider some distinctions between ancient tools and
modern devices, and offer a paradigm for modern life.

I'll start with two stories of digital creation. One evening a few years ago,
my friend Trey asked me how long I thought it would take to read the Bible
straight through. I wasn't sure, but told him that I remembered hearing esti-
mates that if you read the Bible for about ten minutes a day, you'd finish it
in a year. When I got home, I decided to fire up a Bible database to calculate

an exact number for each day of the year. Playing with the data made me wonder if I could create a tool that anyone could use if they wanted to read all or part of the Bible in a given amount of time. This led me to create BibleReadingPlanGenerator.com, a simple website that lets you customize the days, books of the Bible, and format, generating a unique Bible reading plan for you and anyone with whom you want to share it. Once the site was up and running, I posted about it online, and within a few hours several friends reposted the link on their blogs and favorite social media platforms. Within a day or two, thousands of people had visited the site, and I still enjoy seeing people discover it and be encouraged to develop a habit of meeting God in the Scriptures.

I had another rewarding internet experience that started around the time of the iPad's launch in 2010. At the time, most video on the web required a technology called Flash, but Apple didn't want Flash on their products, so they pushed another standard called HTML5. For web developers, this meant they had to support two programming ecosystems (Flash and HTML5) to make their videos work for people with different browsers and devices. For one of my own projects, I created a little code library that could bridge these two technologies, allowing a developer to just plug in my code and have their videos work everywhere. I released my project, called MediaElement.js, under an open source license (meaning anyone could use it or modify it freely), and it turned out that a lot of developers and big tech companies thought it was helpful. Facebook and Twitter used it in their platforms, and it was adopted into the codebase of WordPress which, at the time of this writing, runs around 40 percent of all websites on the internet. Flash was eventually retired, meaning that there was less need for Media Element.js over the years, but for more than a decade, my little side project was probably used to play billions of videos.

These stories illustrate why I love being a part of internet culture and feel blessed to be working in the web development world. The ability to instantly share information and create things that people all over the world can use is, in part, why this is a very interesting time in which to live. At the same time, not all my internet endeavors have been so successful. I wish

I had stayed with my initial forays into Bitcoin mining, and I wish I had not bought the first version of Google Glass. Yet even in the success stories, there are times when I wonder if my work has actually made the world a better place. I am proud of the Bible software I made that has been used by millions of people in gospel-unfriendly countries, but making video technology easier for developers is less clear. I originally made the tools to play seminary lectures, but I wonder, Am I culpable for the content of videos I made easier to consume, or for the amount of video that people watched? Do the messages I received that said, "Wow, it's neat to see a developer who is open about their Christian faith building things like this," make up for those explicitly or implicitly negative uses? What about when I look at the tracking numbers and feel that my sense of worth is tied to the popularity of my projects?

These questions point to some of the complexities of being a creator (or a user) in the digital age. We can affirm the underlying goodness of digital media as part of what God has given us, but if what we've been saying up to this point is correct, then we should expect that the internet and its related technologies also bring a set of tendencies and a distinct value system that may at times be in conflict with what we value as Christians. Digital technology presents us with powerful new ways to shape the world, but that same power also shapes us and the way we see the world. If used without reflection, that shaping will eventually make its way into our souls and communities, influencing how we see ourselves and others and what we think is important. Many of these effects will be rather innocuous, but we should never underestimate the capacity of our flesh to find ways to use technology for self-serving ends and as a means of distraction from our deep need for a Savior and his body, the Christian community.

We'll start with a phenomenon I am calling the "virtualization of culture" that began with the internet and will continue with newer, emerging technology. After that, we'll draw some distinctions between the ancient world of tools and the modern world of digital devices in order to make some recommendations about technology and the table (i.e., Christian community) in our lives.

Virtualization of Culture

In earlier chapters we explored some definitions of culture, such as Ken Myers's "what we make of the world" and Emil Bruner's "the materialization of meaning." Both definitions suggest that when we use God's power of creativity to make something—art, technology, language, dance, clothing—we are also making meaning.

One of the great challenges for Christians in the digital age is that so much of our culture is no longer "material" in the same sense as it has been for generations. The pandemic of 2020 taught us that it is actually possible for us to live most of our life entirely online, where every element of our life—including places, people, things, and rituals—have a virtual representation. Digital media allows us to connect with friends, collaborate with our colleagues, order anything we need, and even worship together. If we hadn't experienced them before, the pandemic showed us that the tools we had were good, the experiences could be real and rich, we could protect ourselves from disease, and we could reach people who were previously unreachable.

And yet, we also found that when forced to engage in entirely virtual forms of interaction and worship, we were not as happy or healthy as having some level of in-person interaction. We engage digital media with our bodies and minds, but because the experience is mediated, our bodies seem to sense that we are not near the activities, places, and people with which we are interacting. This led us to create terms like "Zoom fatigue" to describe what happens when our bodies are fooled into a false sense of physical presence, and "doomscrolling" for the glued-to-the-screen habits we can fall into when we cannot be together enough. We may have learned that we don't need as much business travel as before or as many in-the-building church events, but those months of lockdowns made us all long to share a meal in a restaurant, hear someone singing next to us inside a church, or feel the embrace of a friend.

The pandemic lockdowns in some ways resembled the Israelites' time in the desert. Recall that when the Israelites were in the desert, displaced from the places, objects, and rituals that had marked their life, they felt a sense of anxiety, disconnection, and disruption. Even though their live of slavery was hard, they found themselves longing for the familiar, or at least for objects and rituals that would help them feel grounded and in control. Rather than wait for the words, images, and patterns that God had planned for them, they made their own golden calf and began to worship it rather than God. It may seem a distant memory now, but in the early days of the pandemic, people around the world looked for rituals to cope with their isolation. They made sourdough starters, bought Peloton bikes, watched *Tiger King*, and played Wordle. But like the Israelites, in the midst of isolation and disruption, many of us struggled to form patterns of life that were spiritually and physically healthy. While we hope to never again experience another lockdown, the digital age presents us with choices about what kind of life we want to construct and what kind of community we want to foster. The Israelites in the desert and pandemic lockdowns taught us that when a people don't have firm anchors in the world, they will often respond by creating patterns of life that may not be healthy. The coming waves of technology promise more virtualization, not less, meaning we will need even more wisdom to navigate the digital world faithfully.

Web3, Blockchain, and the Metaverse

For some tech entrepreneurs, Web3 represents the next major wave of internet innovation, promising entirely new ways of interacting online. Looking back in time, the internet became available to the public in 1995, but as early as 1999, web pioneers began thinking about a shift toward what they called "Web 2.0." Whereas the early internet (Web 1.0) was mostly text-based websites that users would passively consume on their desktop computer, Web 2.0 introduced a more visual internet that emphasized user-generated content, interactivity, and mobile access. This included sites like Wikipedia where users collaborated on definitions instead of relying on information from a company, as well as social media that allowed users to connect with each other and share photos more easily than the individual websites of the early internet. However, for all its promise, Web 2.0 became somewhat of a contradiction. It made the internet easier to use, which was supposed to free information, but in the process, the internet became more centralized, allowing a few large companies to control most of what we do online and know more about us than we want.

Web3 promises to restore the dream of the decentralized internet that allows people to engage with ideas and each other in interesting ways while keeping their personal information safe. Two of the primary technologies that undergird Web3 are blockchain, which makes cryptocurrencies like Bitcoin possible, and virtual reality, which has recently been restyled as the metaverse. Blockchain and VR have both been around for some time, but they have only recently come into the public discourse and regular use enough to warrant our attention. Although it's not yet clear exactly how this will play out, the promise of Web3 offers us a chance to put what we've learned to use, examining how the underlying technology itself works, exploring the possible good and bad uses of that technology, and then considering how the value system embedded in the technology might influence us in non-neutral ways. Putting this in terms of our theological tech tetrad, we will explore intentionally redemptive and rebellious uses, as well as the unintentional side effects that come with the technologies, some of which may turn out to be positive and others which may take decades to unravel and understand.

Virtual Reality. At the time of this writing, it is too early to tell if the term "metaverse" will become a widely adopted term to describe interconnected 3D worlds or if it will go the way of "cyberspace," "World Wide Web," and other phrases we've discarded along the way. VR and 3D worlds have been part of internet technology from the beginning but have tended to be bulky, expensive, and undesirable except to those who enjoy experimenting with new technology. Yet the same was true of computers, cameras, phones, and the internet before they were all shrunk down to something that could fit on our wrist. As Apple, Google, and Meta invest heavily in these technologies, they will likely become more accessible and more common.

The first observation we can make is that while a two-dimensional screen on a computer or phone can display an interactive 3D world, a virtual reality system can make the user feel like they are *in* that world. In addition to allowing an individual VR user to have some exciting experiences, it also allows a group of users to see and interact with one another without the need to post, comment, or like anything. In fact, when Facebook rebranded to Meta, founder Mark Zuckerberg put a heavy emphasis on how his company's products would offer a sense of *presence*. Even before Meta, earlier forms of VR allowed users to see others moving, hear them talking, and experience things together that cannot happen on flat screens. For example, after a VR church service, people can move around and have conversations in small groups, something that cannot happen on a traditional livestream service and which is difficult to do even in a video conference like Zoom.

Similarly, while video tools allow teams of people to work together on some projects like shared documents, VR allows collaboration at a more spatial level, enabling teams to see how big a potential product might feel. From an educational perspective, another interesting feature of VR is that a church or school need not merely replicate a church or classroom as a place to teach; it can instead create environments that match what is being taught, such as Hagar alone in the desert (Gen. 16; 21) or Paul during his shipwreck (Acts 27–28). VR can also be used for therapy to help people face fears within a safe, controlled environment. One can easily imagine other interesting, useful, and even redemptive ways to use VR in education, business, and other spheres. At the same time, it shouldn't be surprising that there are many applications of VR that are morally questionable at best and exploitive or explicitly evil as well. But as we've said, understanding a technology is more than listing out good and bad uses; it requires exploring how any use tends to form us.

As we said earlier, it is important to recognize that a person using VR is not truly "disembodied." Instead, they are embodied in a particular posture, namely one in which the user is covered in sensors and screens, blocking out the physically proximate world in favor of a different world. VR users have extraordinary opportunities to see and experience almost anything, but at the same time, with a full headset on, they are incredibly vulnerable to the world around them, including people who might be physically nearby. It's important to note that people are also emotionally vulnerable inside VR because of the kinds of experiences it enables. On the one hand, a therapist can help someone overcome their fear of heights because the sensation inside VR is so real, but on the other hand, studies have indicated women are less likely to want to try VR because the sensation of another user violating one's body or bodily space can feel painfully real inside VR. Meta and other providers have already begun to introduce concepts like a "personal boundary" to counteract these tendencies.

While VR is already fairly mainstream, the promise of wearable augmented reality (AR) technology that allows a user to see the real world and the VR world at the same time is still fairly limited. But when our technology reaches a point where AR and VR experiences are less bulky and obtrusive, they may become the most powerfully shaping medium yet, because in the form of light, wearable glasses or contacts, there will be a layer of technology quietly mediating all human interaction. It's important to note that, as with social media, the hardware and software that makes this possible will likely continue to be subsidized by advertisers. But with the additional sensors in VR, companies won't merely be able to use the data about what you post and like; they may also be able to use the emotion of your voice and the feelings expressed through your facial expressions and bodily movements.

VR may also bring to fruition a promise embedded in the earliest forms of the internet: that you can be whomever (or whatever) you want to be. Like the early message boards and social networks, you can make your avatar into what you wish you were in other spaces. There are of course situations where this might be helpful, but let us never forget that God's work in the world through his Son and by his Spirit are to transform you into the person he created you to be. The church should be a place that accepts all of God's sons and daughters as they are, not as they feel the need to project themselves.

This brings us back to consider the question, What does it means to be *present*? We've probably all experienced a time when we were physically near another person but did not feel present or connected to them. One or both parties might be distracted by work or school, fuming from something the other just said, or on a device that has their attention. At the same time, we've probably all had a technologically mediated interaction that came at just the right time, where the other person felt palpably present. This reminds us that our humanity is both material and immaterial, body and spirit, but that we are finite creatures that cannot be in all places at once. In an age of devices and distraction, being fully present in body and attention (heart, mind, and soul) is one of the most valuable skills we can cultivate and one of the greatest gifts we can give another. We should still use the full array of technology (cars and planes) and media (letters, texts, and VR) to support our relationships, but we must also do the deep work of being as present and undistracted as possible at every opportunity, resisting the tendencies of self-focus and self-creation inherent in some of our technological patterns.

Blockchain. Although less immediately evident to the average consumer, blockchain technology also represents another major shift in digital technology. Like a traditional database, Blockchain stores information, but it has two fundamental differences. First, the information is stored in groups called blocks that are then linked together, forming its namesake, a blockchain. But where data in a normal database is designed to be changeable, data in a blockchain is permanent and cannot be changed without altering the entire blockchain. The second difference is that, where a traditional database is owned by one person or company and stored only on their computers, a blockchain is copied many times on nodes throughout a computer network and owned by no one entity. Together, these two features ensure that a blockchain cannot be altered, because even if someone attempted to insert false data into their copy of the blockchain, the blockchain is replicated on thousands of other nodes that would overrule the errant changes.

Because no one person, company, or government can control or alter blockchain, it is extremely useful for storing a sequence of transactions. This is why the primary use for blockchain has been new forms of money like Bitcoin and the hundreds of other cryptocurrencies and digital wallets on the market. As it is currently conceived, Web3 is an attempt to rebuild the internet as a more decentralized platform, and blockchain technology is an important component in that vision. Blockchain technology is also used to sell and track digital goods. Most digital media, like images, videos, and 3D models, can easily be copied, but a non-fungible token (NFT) built using blockchain technology permanently verifies who the original owner was. This is where blockchain and metaverse technologies interact, with NFTs allowing users to buy and sell things that only exist in a part of the metaverse.

Like Web 2.0, however, the ethos and values of the metaverse and blockchain are seemingly at odds while also being deeply interconnected and interdependent. Large companies want to create metaverse experiences that help sell goods and advertising, which usually takes place in a top-down, highly controlled manner. Blockchain, on the other hand, promises a new, decentralized form of the internet that is free from government and company control. The internet has long pushed in these two directions, with technologies like http, email, and blockchain being created with decentralization and freedom in mind, and companies attempting to build new, interesting, and profitable products with them that they often feel require more centralization and control for maximal earnings. The important thing to realize in this discussion is that these technologies have been designed with a certain set of values and goals, some intentionally given to them by their creators, and some discovered later in their usage. Sometimes these values align with human interests, and sometimes they create conflicts between companies and communities.

The cryptocurrencies built on blockchain also offer an excellent opportunity to reflect on the meaning inherent in our technology and the social systems we create around them. After the technology of language and the alphabet, money is perhaps the next most powerful invention of humanity (and one of the most often-mentioned subjects in the Scriptures). When humans barter, they trade physical goods or services directly, such as an apple for ten nuts or a stack of wood for help building a house. But as the number of tradable items grows, a need arises for an intermediary that can be easily reproduced, such as coins or bills. Currency works by swapping the physical process of bartering for a "virtual" process where money represents the value of physical goods. But for currency to work, there must be a centralized authority to ensure its ongoing value. Thus, in the case of money, a government is quite literally imbuing a round piece of metal or a rectangular piece of paper with a value system. Jesus himself references this authority when he says, "Give back to Caesar what is Caesar's" (Mark 12:17). On the one hand, having a central authority controlling the value of money makes it universally useful. And yet, the centralization of value is also what usually means that richer people are able to take advantages of complex economic forces like inflation to gain more wealth, while those same forces disproportionality affect poor people, preventing them from gaining more financial independence.

In theory, cryptocurrencies promise a fairer and more democratized form of currency because their value cannot be controlled in this way by governments or companies. In practice, however, cryptocurrency value currently often fluctuates and tends to be much more volatile than traditional currencies. The human bent toward greed and selfishness also comes into conflict with the democratic values that cryptocurrency founders attempted to build in. Though some companies are trying to build helpful products on top of blockchain, many other aspects of the crypto market seem to focus on speculation designed only for wealth accumulation rather than societal good. Another potential issue is that cryptocurrency has the traceability of earlier forms of electronic money like credit cards, but also the anonymity of cash. On the positive side, this allows people to send cryptocurrency across country lines without paying high fees or being subject to inflationary controls, but on the other hand, it enables bad actors to hide illegal or abusive transactions. Maintaining and growing cryptocurrency also uses enormous amounts of energy, possibly causing more harm to creation than good for humanity. But however it is used, it is important to remember that cryptocurrency is not merely a technology; it is an ideology and a system of values that requires careful thought.

In this discussion of virtual reality and block technology, my hope is that we are learning how to study the way a new technology works, what it might be used for, and the inherent values embedded in it, some of which may be obvious and some of which are more subtle. New technology often comes with a promise of a better world, and Web3 promises to fix some of the problems with Web 2.0. But we need to remember that Web 2.0 was supposed to make the original internet a much better, freer, happier place. In some ways, Web 2.0 succeeded in bringing people around the world together, but in others ways it failed more spectacularly than even the most skeptical pundit would have predicted. In other words, if the results of several decades of social media are any indication, we should be very skeptical of Web3's claim of a blockchain-enabled metaverse utopia. Still, we are not called to retreat from this world, but to live faithfully within it, so let us press on to understand more of the digital world.

The Device Paradigm

As we consider these vast changes, it can be challenging to chart a clear way forward. But even before the digital era, Christian thinkers have attempted to capture what makes the modern era of technology so exciting and yet difficult to grapple with. One such thinker was philosopher Albert Borgmann, who, in his book *Technology and the Character of Contemporary Life*, identified a phenomenon he called "the device paradigm" to describe some of the ways in which modern technology can create a fast-paced and yet sometimes unsatisfying world.[1]

Borgmann uses the word *device* in a very specific sense to refer to a tool that takes a long, difficult process for a human and makes it available at the press of a button or the flip of a switch. For example, 150 years ago, heating a home required going outside, finding trees, cutting them down, chopping the wood, bringing the wood inside, and starting a fire in the fireplace. This process would take significant time, and keeping the fire going would require skill and practice. But today the commodity of heat is available at the press of a button through a device. Most of us don't think about where it comes from or how it works, because even a child can operate a thermostat.

Of course, Borgmann would say that this readily available heat is a good thing that often saves lives. But he points out that the device is also doing something we don't notice: it is hiding the process of making heat. We press a button and heat comes out, but we don't know what goes on inside our walls or underneath our houses, and we no longer go about the practice of making heat ourselves. Why does this matter? The answer is that when a device hides a process, sometimes we lose out on (or in McLuhan's terms, amputate) an important part of human life.

I encountered this firsthand when I first moved to Dallas several years ago. Some friends invited me to live with them in a hundred-year-old historic house with a beautiful porch around three sides of its structure. My roommates and I always talked about how great it would be to just sit out on the porch and hang out together, but we never really found the time. One day I ran into a man who was renovating one of the historic homes, and he told me that back when these houses were first built, everyone in the neighborhood used to be out on their porches. On hot summer afternoons, families would sit out on the porch, letting the breeze cool them off as they drank lemonade and shared stories about the day. But this changed when everyone installed air conditioners in their homes. Once cool air was available at the press of a button, they no longer needed to go outside to cool off. The device had hidden the process of cooling that used to take place outside, and the result was that the space where people used to commune became obsolete. Over time, as people spent more time indoors, neighbors became strangers.

Borgmann's point is not to say that we should get rid of our heating or cooling devices, but that we should be careful to notice the processes and practices our devices hide and the humanity that is sometimes lost at the same time. Take, for example, the difference between cooking a lasagna from scratch and ordering lasagna to be delivered. The device paradigm is operating here because both the process of preparing a meal and the practice of eating it together at the table have been compressed down into what we call "fast food." Again, the point is not that fast food is inherently bad (although that might be true); the point is that, in compressing these human practices down into a commodity available at the press of a button, the space for human connection, meaning, and depth is often lost. In chapter

8, we saw that after Jesus's resurrection, he took time to prepare a meal for Peter to set the context for his restoration (John 21:9). But imagine how different Peter would have felt if Jesus had used Uber Eats to deliver a Big Mac with a printed message saying, "You're all good. Get back at it."

Going beyond Borgmann's initial work, it is not difficult to see how social media functions as a "device" in the sense that it takes a human process and turns it into a commodity that can be consumed on demand. Our relationships, communication, inside jokes, and even movie-watching are all available at the press of a button without going through some of the processes that would be common before the internet. Growing followers, likes, and views all take work, but this takes place through a very different meaning-making process than deepening individual relationships and loving our actual neighbors.

From Tools to Devices

Before we get to Borgmann's alternative to the device paradigm, let us spend some time expanding on the differences between older tools and modern devices. In this book, we've been using a broad definition of technology that covers a broad array of items we can group into two categories: older *tools*, like hammers and aqueducts, and modern tools we call *devices*, like phones and VR headsets. This helps us affirm that all human creations are good gifts from God and that they transform us as we use them. Although hammers and phones both fall under the umbrella of technology, below I have outlined some important distinctions between them that can help us see the unique challenges and opportunities of the digital age.

Physical to Mental/Spiritual. One of the clearest distinctions between an older tool and a modern device is that most ancient tools are designed to extend our physical abilities while electronic devices tend to extend our mental capacities. Hammers extend our arms, telescopes our eyes, and microphones our voices. But starting with computers, we interact with devices primarily on a mental level, accessing information that affects what we know and believe.

Writing was humankind's first mental technology because it allowed humans to offload their knowledge and share it with others without being nearby one another. In a sense, digital technology, from websites to spreadsheets, can be seen as more powerful versions of writing. And yet, we also recognize that digital media encompasses much more than simply advanced writing. We use our phones not just for information or communication but as a way of being in the world. Modern devices connect deep into our interiority as we connect and share with friends, record important moments, map our surroundings, and pay for goods. These activities engage our minds and even reach into our souls.

Self-Contained to Dependent. Another way to think of the difference between tools and devices is to consider their power source. Does the technology require human or animal strength, or does the technology require another technology to function? We consider desks, pots, doors, pipes, and mechanical clocks to be tools because their primary function is contained within their parts, and any power they require comes from human input. Modern devices, on the other hand, are usually dependent on power and connection to other technologies, like batteries and the internet, to be of use.

Humans were created to make tools, and in some sense, human life is dependent on them. How long could any of us survive without clothing, shelter, and a means of acquiring food? Today we've also become increasingly dependent on devices that are themselves dependent on a vast array of other technology and power consumption. We even purchase battery packs for our phones just to make sure we don't lose connection for more than a few minutes. This leads us to consider two things: first, the relationship of our technological dependencies and our dependence on God, and second, the importance of fasting from good things that can draw our attention away from God.

Single to Multipurpose. Older tools also tend to have a single, focused function. Think of screwdrivers, saws, colanders, vacuums, and so on, whose function and purpose are often immediately clear. Then consider how phones and computers have nearly limitless potential for creation and consumption. The keyboard on a computer favors typing, but tablets and phones have almost no predefined interface other than a screen, which is a blank slate for developers and creators.

This multipurpose nature of modern devices does several important things. First, on the positive end, it affords amazing possibilities for creating, collaborating, and experiencing whatever someone can imagine. At the same time, this lack of clear purpose creates a phenomenon we can call *teleological ambiguity*—the unclear goal or purpose of something. When we pick up a tool, we usually already have a goal in mind, but sometimes we pick up a screen out of habit and then see what it directs us toward. A third important point is that teleological ambiguity means those around us often can't tell what we're doing with a device. If they see us holding a measuring cup, they might guess we are cooking, but if they see us hunched over a phone, it could mean anything. Kids grow up seeing their parents in front of a computer, but it is difficult for them to understand what their parents do all day with the machine they also use for watching shows or playing games. But this isn't just a challenge for parents. Indeed, all of us could do more to reflect on what is truly driving our device usage.

Linear to Logarithmic. Building on the previous point, a tool only enables its user to do one thing at a time—carve a stick, play a song, beat an egg. We can mechanize those tools to allow us to increase the output, but this increase tends to be linear (for example, measured in "horsepower"). However, unlike a tool, a device's power can quickly multiply as it connects with other devices, giving us control over many things at once and, in some cases, leading to logarithmic or exponential change.

A simple example might be home automation systems that empower everything in and outside a house. But we can see a more complex version of this with Silicon Valley's outsized influence over American and world culture. Technologists know how to scale products, taking advantage of network effects to optimize the technology they are building toward whatever end goal their company might have. The immense influence of new technology over culture and everyday processes mean that as more people adopt a product, it becomes harder for everyone else not to. This creates a kind of inevitability around technological progress, which means there is always a place for Christian technologists to contribute to discussions about which technologies should exist, and to help us live faithfully in an era where we cannot control all that is happening.

Extend to Replace. Earlier, we explored McLuhan's idea that a technology can be understood by how it *extends* our natural ability. But if a tool *extends* what we do, we can say that in some cases a device *replaces* something we might have done. If a broom or vacuum cleaner extends our ability to clean, making it faster and more efficient, a robot vacuum cleaner replaces that activity altogether. In other words, a tool helps you do something, but a device does something for you.

In addition to affecting the kinds of things we do as individuals, this also affects people we interact with and their jobs. For example, grocery stores first replaced their checkout stations with self-scanners, and then the pandemic helped grocery delivery become more popular, allowing us to outsource the entire trip to the store. In related ways, jobs in assembly, transportation, medicine, law, and education will continue to change as devices such as robots and AI do more menial, repetitive tasks for us but also require people to adjust.

Another way of considering the "tools extend, devices replace" difference comes in the form of body modification. Instead of developing tools that our body uses, we are developing devices that can be implanted in our bodies, from pacemakers to bionic limbs that replace what was damaged or lost. An important question is, Should we limit this kind of replacement to restoring functionality that was lost, or is upgrading beyond normal human capacity acceptable?

Maintainable to Replaceable. Tools often require some form of ongoing maintenance to keep them in optimal working conditions. Pianos and guitars must be tuned, and cars require regularly replacing fluids, tires, and other parts that wear out. But most modern devices don't have any way to maintain them, at least in the physical sense. A modern phone or tablet is a stunning feat of hardware and software engineering, but the parts are so intricate that they often can't be replaced or updated.

Some tech critics have urged Apple and other tech companies to make their devices more repairable by end users, but these companies usually say that repairability would make them larger and more expensive. Some computers still allow parts to be exchanged or upgraded, but most devices need to be entirely replaced once they have worn out. While it is nice when something "just works," we must also be careful not to create so much waste that we violate God's command to cultivate and care for the earth. We may also find that maintaining some older tools can be a restorative process for ourselves as we see the possibility of the restoration of all things.

Inert to Persuasive. We have previously said that when most people think of the word *technology*, they mean an internet-connected device of some kind, in contrast to tools that aren't digital or connected. We are so used to internet connection today that we only notice it when it fails. But we must also acknowledge that connectivity radically shapes our relationship to a device because it opens us up to people who often have a vested interest in directing how we use it.

For example, your shovel is not connected to people with PhDs in persuasive computing who are researching how to get you to dig another hole. But your phone and its apps connect you to a network of thousands of engineers, whose job it is to find a way to get you to watch another video, play another level, or scroll through more posts, all in hopes of showing you an ad that will get you to do or buy something. This connectivity also allows us to know the weather at the time we land in another city, reroute our commute around traffic, and adjust the temperature of our coffee or air conditioner from afar, but these services are generally paid for either in monthly fees or in advertising (which is designed to draw our attention). Another way of describing the contrast between inert and persuasive is to say that tools are usually acquired through a direct transaction or one-time payment, while devices are funded through ongoing services, usually paid for by marketers and data miners. This reality means we must continually ask ourselves about what we value in life, and whether staying connected is important or if relying on disconnected tools for a time might be more life-giving.

Effort to Attention. Returning to the example of an instrument, a room with a piano invites us into the effort of learning to play, which can last a lifetime. In contrast, a room with a television invites us to give our attention to effortless consumption. Sometimes we marvel at a child who quickly intuits how a device works, and yet this is how devices are designed—to require almost no effort, prior experience, or training. A tablet can draw the youngster's attention with lights and sounds, but it doesn't require the effort of stacking blocks or coloring inside the lines. Similarly, almost all the apps on our phones are built to get our attention and then keep it through notifications, social feedback, and content algorithms. The more attention we give, the more our phone learns what we want, and the feedback loop can intensify.

But attention is also key for creating things with digital media, which often requires intense concentration and focus. Learning to code isn't terribly hard, but learning to code well requires constant training and adapting to an ever-changing world of standards and devices. Likewise, digital design and art also invite effort and an iterative process that learns from previous errors or user feedback. At the same time, there is a tutorial crutch that can happen where people watch more cooking, woodworking, or design videos than they actually do those things, sucked in by the attention rather than giving the effort. For us to grow and develop as people, we need to give ourselves to things that require effort, like learning a new skill, considering deep ethical questions, or learning to listen and be present.

Presence to Connection. Since the advent of writing (an older tool), people have been able to communicate with each other across time and space. But real-time mediums on modern devices move us beyond communication to connection. Digital technology allows us to connect with one another in almost limitless ways, offering amazing possibilities for education, business, church, and relationships. Rather than mailing artwork to grandparents, children can conduct a live show-and-tell halfway around the world. Rather than travelling around the world on a speaking tour, authors can connect with more audiences online for a fraction of the cost. Rather than listen to a recorded sermon, a person who is disabled at home or living far from a church can worship simultaneously with other believers.

But these opportunities for connection also alter how we understand presence. For all its incredible value, being digitally connected is not the same as being physically present. Moreover, when we are connected to a faraway person through a device, we often find ourselves disconnected from those physically nearby. In other words, we can be materially present but spiritually disconnected. At every level, from business to church to relationships, we need to carefully consider when to be connected digitally and when our tangible presence is more valuable, however costly it might be.

Creating to Remixing. One of the key features of "new media" or "digital media" is the way it enables us to share and remix material. Remix culture is most often associated with music, where instead of recording raw instruments and voices, newer forms of music are created and mixed synthetically using prerecorded and computer-generated sounds along with autotuned voices. But remix culture can be found in all kinds of creative endeavors. In the world of programming, we constantly reuse and reshape code examples and libraries made by others. Remixing is everywhere, including 3D modeling and printing, stock photography and video, and even TikTok trends, all of which unlock amazing new creative expressions and potential.

As with the other categories above, there is no clear line between creating from scratch and remixing, but understood broadly, both have unique meaning and significance for us. Sometimes going back a layer in our creating can be a meaningful practice. For example, a coffee lover might try roasting her own beans, or a painter might make his own colors. At the same time, taking something good and adding your own twist can be a rich experience of participating in communal meaning-making. Thinking theologically, everything we do is a kind of remixing of God's good creation. He alone creates from nothing, and we cocreate from what he has made.

Focal Practices

Clearly, the modern world of devices is different from the world of tools just a few generations ago. How, then, can we live faithfully and not be taken over by the machines? For his part, Borgmann does not think the proper response to the device paradigm is to turn off our heaters, throw out our microwaves, or delete the latest social app from our phones. Instead, he recommends that we take time to intentionally establish what he called "focal things" and "focal practices." Focal practices are activities that technology can do for us but that we choose to do anyway because it affords us the kind of life we value.

For example, cars, motorcycles, and Segways make walking or running long distances completely unnecessary. Yet the practice of running a long distance keeps our bodies healthy and can bring calm to our hectic lives. In the language of Genesis, running helps us balance our "cultivating" of the garden with our "keeping" of it and helps restore the equilibrium between natural and unnatural. Similarly, it's not practical for most of us to make a lasagna from scratch every night, but for many people the chance to prepare a meal can be a deeply restorative practice and one that invites connection with other human beings. The food and the oven become "focal things" where our humanity can be recentered and reoriented to the world God made.

Borgmann also concentrates his writing on the practice of the Lord's Supper found in the New Testament. Fundamental to the life of the early church was the preparation and sharing of a meal around a table. The table itself became a focal thing, a place around which people gathered to share life and encourage each other in faith. Instead of living our lives according to the values of new technology, Borgmann urges us to determine what our values are first, and to attempt to use our tools in service of those values. As the speed of the world increases, the practice of Communion may be one of the most countercultural practices Christians can regularly engage in to express and embody their values. Many Christian traditions only practice Communion monthly or quarterly, but in the digital age, Communion may be one of the most important weekly practices we can do together.

Optimize for the Table

A final concept from the tech world can draw these ideas together in the way we live our lives. Technology entrepreneurs often talk about their products in terms of what they are optimized for. A good product can't do everything well, so companies need to intentionally make choices that favor (or optimize) one outcome, knowing that they might not achieve others. For example, one company might optimize for customer satisfaction while another optimizes for a lower cost of operation.

The question "What are you optimizing for?" can be applied beyond tech companies into our lives and ministries. Whether we intend it or not, the choices we make every day are optimized for some outcome. If even we don't think of ourselves as being very "optimal" or efficient, that might mean we've arranged (i.e., optimized) our lives for a carefree lifestyle with few responsibilities or time commitments. Upon reflection, others may realize that their life is optimized in a direction that is in conflict with what they believe or value. A person might say they value spending time with friends or engaging in a hobby, but in reality, the number of hours they work is optimizing for something else. Borgmann's concern, and ours in this book, is how to optimize our lives in such a way that is most congruent with the image bearing God has called us to. Rather than see technology as an enemy toward this end, it can play an important role in moving us toward this vision.

My wife and I recently attempted to adjust what we were optimized for in a small way, and it's had a big impact on our lives. When we first married, we bought a beautiful eight-person bar table for our home. Everyone who came over commented on how great it looked in our dining room. Unfortunately, it wasn't very comfortable, and we found ourselves spending very little time there. As our family grew, we had trouble establishing mealtime as an important part of our lives. So recently, we decided to sell the pretty table for a more functional and comfortable one that we can sit at for hours with our children and friends. We did this because we have chosen to place a high value on the time we spend together, and although our technological culture urges us to go faster and faster, we work against those values every time we intentionally gather around the dinner table as a focal thing. We use technology like phones and social media to invite friends over, but we are trying to use our devices in a way that is optimized for the table.

I've seen my kids do this in some amazing ways as they've grown older. We've attempted to instill in them the idea that screens are for making, not just consuming, and they each have learned to optimize their screen usages for creation. My son tends toward programming, video editing, and 3D modeling, and he and his friends spend much of their time together online planning the next hilarious video. My daughter bears God's image in different ways, using her computer to make flyers for neighborhood talent shows or to design her latest contraption (which might just be a pully system for opening and closing doors from her bed). In their own way, according to the unique ways God has wired them, my kids have found ways to direct their tools and devices toward connection, engagement, fun, and joy.

We've also found that optimizing for family connection sometimes means setting limits on certain technology. When my wife and I come home from work, we attempt to reserve several hours where the phone and computers are placed out of reach. This serves to carve a space out of the day (or as Borgmann calls it, a focal place) where we can interact and share meals as a family. As my kids grow older, it has become increasingly challenging to put our devices away at the same time. But we are all optimizing for something, right? What we've found is that when we are all disconnected from the outer world for a time, it frees us up to be fully present with the people right in front of us.

The guiding principle is this: technology is for the table. In other words, everything we do with our tools—scheduling appointments on our phones, heating up meals in the microwave, reading updates from friends and family on social media—should all be directed toward enriching the few, precious face-to-face encounters we have in our busy world.

Here's a simple example of how this might work: pull out your phone, schedule an appointment with a friend you haven't seen in a while, and in the meantime take a look at their social profile to see what's happening in their life. Rather than being jealous of their trips or reacting to their political views, think about what's going on behind what he or she is saying online. When you do meet, you won't have to spend as much time getting updated on what's happened since the last time you were together, allowing you to move more easily into deeper communion with one another. Used in this way, your calendar and social media are being directed (or optimized) toward the table, and hopefully they will increase your chances of experiencing the "complete joy" that John wanted to have with his fellow believers.

I wish I could say that I do this every time I meet with people. And I wish I could say every evening between 5:00 p.m. and 8:00 p.m. is the best time of my life, when the screens are off, the flowers bloom, and my family sings in perfect tune. But marriage, parenting, and friendships can be difficult at times, and often I would rather check my stats and see how many people have congratulated me online for something I made or said. But I don't like the person I become when I spend all my time online, any more than I like the person I become when I spend all my time eating fast food. Instead, I know that it is often the difficult things—eating healthy food and exercising, reading books for long periods, praying deeply, and spending quality time with my family and friends—that God uses to mold and shape me into the image of his Son. Rather than be shaped by technology, I try to understand how each new technology can shape me and then decide if that coincides with the kind of person I think God would have me be and the kind of community he wants us to create.

QUESTIONS

- What are some important events, rituals, or communications (e.g., meetings, sports, church worship, donations) that you used to do in person that you now do primarily in a digital format? How has that benefitted or detracted from the events?
- Of the contrasts between older tools and modern devices presented here, which are most helpful to you, and which present the biggest challenges for the kind of life you want to live?
- What are some focal places and practices that help ground you in the values you hold?
- What are you optimizing for?

RECOMMENDATIONS

IF I'VE BEEN SUCCESSFUL in this book, I will have convinced you that technology is, as I've called it, "a God-given transformative force." In the grand story of Scripture, God has charged us, his image bearers, with the responsibility to cultivate and keep his garden, and we use tools to fulfill that command. This means that, theologically speaking, technology in its nature is something that God calls "good." And yet we have also seen that the tools we are called to use to transform God's creation also transform us. From the shovel that reshapes our hands, arms, and minds to the phone that modifies our conception of space, friendship, and wilderness, every tool shapes the world and reshapes its user. In addition, our tools are powerful conveyers of meaning and values that have the capacity to shape our souls and relationships. Rather than labelling technology "neutral" (as I once thought), focusing only on what we do with it, we should view technology as a good gift from God and a powerful force of transformation that sometimes brings unintended consequences.

According to the biblical story, we live in the time between the garden

and the city, anticipating Christ's return when he will make all things
new—including our souls, our bodies, our planet, and even some of the
things we've made. We recognize that technology has a powerful yet limited
redemptive capacity, and that it also has corruptive tendencies. It offers foretastes of the coming kingdom of God when all things will be made right,
but it can also serve as a replacement god that promises another form of
transcendence. How then should the Christian live in a technological age?
How can we "seek the welfare of the city" (Jer. 29:7 ESV) without giving in
to its downsides?

One approach is to avoid all new technology and attempt to go as far
backward in time as possible, to the age when things seemed to be simpler
and better. While this approach is at times tempting, we must remember that
we've not been called to go backward in time but to live faithfully in our own
age. At the other extreme, we might argue that we should use technology as
much and as often as we can, not worrying about its problems because at
Christ's return he will remake all things, including our problematic technology. But this forward-looking approach will similarly fail the test of living
faithfully with what we've been given.

At the conclusion of his book, David Hopper writes, "The challenge to
theology of technology's coming of age is for theology to affirm its own
proper counterproject of life-in-community. . . . It must speak from isness
and not . . . from the perspective of some 'final hope.'"[1] Hopper is saying
that Christians cannot be content merely to criticize technology on the one
hand, nor to simply look toward Christ's return on the other. Instead, the
Christian community must begin from what God has called it to be—its
"isness"—and live out of that. Only from that position can we faithfully
approach and cautiously use technology. To see how this might practically
work out, I would recommend five steps: valuation, experimentation, limitation, togetherness, and cultivation.

Valuation. We must begin by continually returning to the Scriptures to find
our Christian values and identity. From that perspective we can evaluate
the strengths and weaknesses of technology and determine which values

will emerge from the tendencies of use built into its design. In the appendix you'll find a set of questions based on what we learned from the biblical story. This is designed to help surface these patterns and emergent values in the things we create and use. After going through this evaluation process, we can ask where our Christian values and the values of technology might be in conflict, and which aspects of the tool our flesh will be tempted to use in ways that do not honor God.

For example, the New Testament repeatedly affirms the fullness and completeness that only comes from being physically together, sharing embodied, face-to-face interaction. Phones, however, can only enable distanced communication, and they tend to value being connected to those who are physically absent rather than those who are nearby. Phones are still helpful and useful and even redemptive in some cases, but in order to have the fullness of Christian community, we must work both through and against the value system of the phone. Use them to get together, use them to share funny videos, but don't let them have dominion over your time together.

Experimentation. Thinking critically about technology is helpful, but it's difficult to discover the tendencies and value systems built into a technology without actually using it. A controlled experiment in using a tool can help us discover things that we can only know through experience. For example, I tried making a newspaper my only source of news for a few weeks. Instead of watching TV, listening to the radio, or using my phone, I bought a paper every day for two weeks to see what would happen. The differences were staggering. I found that I treated news differently when I paid for it, and that I was exposed to stories I normally wouldn't have seen online. I also found it difficult to take a news break at work since everyone could see me pull out the newspaper, whereas no one noticed when I opened up a browser tab to a news website.

Most technology creators have an iterative process for trying new versions of their products, experimenting with what works and how their clients respond. A church could take on this model by intentionally experimenting with the amount of media, the size of their band, the lighting in the room,

and so on, carefully noting what differences in meaning emerged. Individuals can try things like handwriting notes to friends or learning a new social
media platform to discover what it means to use it. Although one does not
necessarily have to use a technology to understand it, a good experiment can
do something even more important—it can help a person from one techno-
culture understand the people who live in another techno-culture.

Limitation. Once we understand the patterns of usage of a technology, the
next step is to see what happens when we put boundaries on it. Recall that
God himself embedded the pattern of rest in his creation, both as a celebration of his work and for the Israelites to remember their freedom. Similarly,
if we realize that spending too much time on social media invites narcis-
sism, and that reading online too much limits deep thinking, we may not
be living in the freedom of Sabbath, and we may need to reinstitute some
limits. It is here that the desires of the flesh often emerge most strongly. A
person who checks his or her phone regularly throughout the day may find
it extremely difficult to curtail this pattern.

Because of this difficulty, incorporating a technology fast or Sabbath
into one's mental diet can be particularly helpful. It is, of course, somewhat
misleading to call it a fast since we're still using twentieth-century tools like
lights, air-conditioning, and vehicles; but choosing to abstain for several
days from the tools that impact us most powerfully can help weaken their
control. In my profession, I've found it difficult to disconnect for several
days at a time, so instead I try to make disconnection a regular part of every
day. I've also found that using alarms on my phone in the morning means
I am much more likely to start the day checking my feeds. So I bought a
cheap alarm clock and put my phone on a charger in another room to help
me reorient the start of my day. My goal is not simply to limit my technology usage but to open up space to live the kind of life Christ modeled for
us and the Sabbath freedom he earned for us. When I feel the urge to go
outside these boundaries, I have to ask myself if I'm doing so out of my
Christian values and identity or if I'm being pulled into the value system of
technology.

Togetherness. The previous three steps—valuation, experimentation, and limitation—will be rendered mostly useless if we practice them in isolation apart from the context of Christian fellowship. An interesting example of making community-based technology decisions can be found in Eric Brende's book *Better Off*, in which he describes living for eighteen months in a small, technologically minimalist community very similar to an Amish village. In one story, the entire community came together to discuss the pros and cons of installing a single phone in their midst.[2] Another example of a group-oriented technology decision came when a group of trapped Chilean miners decided not to allow personal music players or video games to be lowered down to them because they determined that "those tend to isolate people from one another."[3]

Today's technology places a high value on personalization, customization, and the preferences of the individual. That made the decision of the Chilean miners to value the needs of the group over the desires of the individuals a radical departure from the value system of technological society. Anytime we choose to do technology together rather than as individuals, we are rejecting the self-centered orientation of the flesh and choosing to work out the togetherness portrayed in the Scripture and within the triune God. Also, finding a balance of community online and offline can be important and help us avoid becoming too deeply ingrained into unhealthy ideologies that tend to spread more quickly online.

Cultivation. Finally, in our attempts to approach technology with discernment, we must be careful not to enter into a kind of inactive stasis where we talk about technology but fail to support those who are actually *doing* technology in service of what God has asked of his image bearers: to cultivate and keep his creation and to make disciples of all nations.

In recent years, Christian communities have been rediscovering the importance of cultivating and nurturing artists, and I think the time has come for us to begin doing the same with those working in technology. We already spend time and resources developing and encouraging business people and politicians, yet it is the technologists—the men and women creating the next generation of tools—who are often implicitly making important decisions about health care, energy, internet regulation, privacy, weapons availability, biomedical advances, artificial intelligence, and so on. We are not all called to be inventors, but we can work toward helping technologists think theologically and Christianly about what they are making. I hope that this book is a helpful starting point for doing this.

If there is one final recommendation I can give in regard to technology, it is that we attempt to do something like what this book has done. We looked at the story of Scripture through the lens of technology in order that we might view technology through the lens of the story of God and his people, with the resurrected Christ at beginning, middle, and end of that story. It is his life, work, and promises that should inform our value system, shape the way we see the world, and transform the way we live in it.

It is my hope that the biblical and philosophical tools presented in this book will help us become better stewards of the technological tools God has entrusted to us, as we seek to live lives that honor him and the work of his Son. And on our journey from the garden to the city, I pray that we never confuse the city for the Savior, but instead work toward the vision of the heavenly city with the Savior seated on his throne surrounded by the Tree of Life, the River of Life, his redeemed people, and their restored creations.

Appendix

THEOLOGICAL TECHNOLOGY TETRAD

BELOW IS THE CHART from chapter 9 that brings together the four parts of the biblical story—creation, fall, redemption, and restoration—in a way that allows us to consider positive, negative, intentional, and unintentional aspects of technology. After this chart, you'll find questions that you can ask in groups to help surface issues about any technology you might want to consider.

	Positive	Negative
Intentional	3. Redemption	2. Rebellion
Unintentional	1. Reflection	4. Restoration

Reflection (Unintentionally Positive)

- What unique aspects of God's nature does this technology reflect?
- What aspects of our human nature does this technology enhance and extend?
- How does this technology help accomplish the creation mandate to cultivate the earth and create from it?
- Is this technology more practically oriented (used to accomplish a task), or does it exist for its own sake (to be beautiful)?
- Is this tool primarily used to *create* new things, or is it used primarily to *consume* things that exist?
- What patterns of behavior have emerged over time as this technology has taken hold in society?
- What actions, thoughts, and social structures does this technology value or favor?

Rebellion (Intentionally Negative)

- What obvious negative uses of this technology do you know of?
- What embedded values does this technology have that are in conflict with a biblical portrait of humanity, justice, and peace?
- What aspects of this technology's power will our flesh be tempted to exploit (Gal. 5:17; James 1:13–15)?
- In what ways could this technology reinforce the myth that we can live apart from dependence upon God (Gen. 4:17; Isa. 40:18–20)?
- What will happen if we use this technology too much (Eph. 5:18)?
- What limits can we place on using this technology to prevent it from using us (Mark 9:43; Heb. 12:1)?

Redemption (Intentionally Positive)

- What effects of the fall can this technology help to overcome (Gen. 3:7; 1 Tim. 5:23)?
- Is this technology primarily designed for entertainment and fun (e.g., video games) or does it have a greater significance (e.g., cochlear implants)?

- What embedded values does this technology have that are a complement to the biblical image of humanity and the church?
- How can this technology be used to accomplish Jesus's commands to help the less fortunate (Matt. 25:34–40)?
- How does this technology point toward the final redemption that Christ has promised?

Restoration (Unintentionally Negative)

- What unintended consequences, shortcomings, or trade-offs does this technology bring?
- Is it possible to use the technology in a different way to avoid these problems? If not, how does the presence of such problems help us long for the future restoration of all things through Christ?
- Do the benefits of this technology outweigh its shortcomings?
- Is this technology funded by selling personal data? Is there another business model that could make it profitable without being exploitative?
- How do you imagine God would make this technology better in the new city?
- What creative ways can you contribute to making this technology better?

NOTES

Chapter 1: Perspective

1. This quote is widely attributed to Alan Kay (sometimes in the alternate form, "Technology is anything that wasn't around when you were born"), but no specific source has been provided. The closest reference I could find was possibly from a Hong Kong press conference in the 1980s.

2. John Dyer, *The People of the Screen: How Evangelicals Created the Digital Bible and How It Shapes the Way We Read Scripture* (New York: Oxford University Press, 2022).

3. To describe this phenomenon, Tom Pettitt coined the term "Gutenberg parenthesis" in a lecture given at the international conference of Media in Transition (April 2007). See "Before the Gutenberg Parenthesis: Elizabethan-American Compatibilities," http://web.mit.edu/comm-forum/mit5/papers/pettitt_plenary_gutenberg.pdf.

4. Neil Postman, "Five Things We Need to Know About Technological Change" (lecture, Denver, CO, March 28, 1998), https://web.cs.ucdavis.edu/~rogaway/classes/188/materials/postman.pdf.

5. Arthur C. Clarke, "Hazards of Prophecy: The Failure of Imagination,"

in *Profiles of the Future: An Enquiry into the Limits of the Possible*, rev. ed. (New York: Henry Holt & Co, 1984), 36.

6. Jamais Cascio, "Your Posthumanism Is Boring Me," Gizmodo, May 8, 2010, https://gizmodo.com/your-posthumanism-is-boring-me-553 3833.

7. Douglas Adams, "How to Stop Worrying and Learn to Love the Internet," September 1, 1999, http://www.douglasadams.com/dna/199909 01-00-a.html.

8. Hilary Stout, "How Does Technology Affect Kids' Friendships?" *New York Times*, posted April 30, 2010 (print edition May 2, 2010), http://www.nytimes.com/2010/05/02/fashion/02BEST.html.

9. The plural of *medium* in this sense is usually *media*, which means that *mediums* is unconventional, if not outright grammatically incorrect. However, because the word *media* is often associated with "news media" and "the media," I have opted for *mediums* as the plural of *medium*.

10. Other works go deeper into such issues. For example, Jack Swearengen, a former nuclear scientist, explored far-reaching implications of nuclear technology in *Beyond Paradise: Technology and the Kingdom of God* (Eugene, OR: Wipf & Stock, 2007); and Brian Brock offers a deeper look into the theology and philosophy of technology and offers guidance on applying it to modern issues in *Christian Ethics in a Technological Age* (Grand Rapids: Eerdmans, 2010).

11. Arthur Boers, *Living into Focus: Choosing What Matters in an Age of Distractions* (Grand Rapids: Brazos, 2012), ch. 5.

12. Thankfully, Socrates's student Plato recorded many of Socrates's best dialogues, preserving his thoughts for the ages. One of the stories Plato preserved for us is called *Phaedrus*, in which Socrates shared his concerns about the written word. He did this by telling his students the legend of the Egyptian god Theuth who offered the gift of writing to King Thamus. Theuth believed writing would be a remedy for bad memories, but King Thamus objected, saying that the true result would be creating people who had only the appearance of wisdom.

13. Heidi A. Campbell, "Understanding the Relationship between Religion Online and Offline in a Networked Society," *Journal of the American Academy of Religion* 80, no. 1 (March 2012): 64–93.

Chapter 2: Imagination

1. David Nye, *Technology Matters: Questions to Live With* (Cambridge, MA: MIT Press, 2007), 3.
2. Egbert Schuurman, *Faith and Hope in Technology* (Toronto: Clements, 2003), 64–65.
3. David A. Mindell, "Cultural Impacts of Technology," *Wiley Encyclopedia of Electrical and Electronics Engineering*, ed. John G. Webster (Hoboken, NJ: John Wiley & Sons, 1999), 1, doi:10.1002/047134608X .W7301. Thanks to Dr. Merritt Roe Smith for helping me track this down.
4. For the use of the shovel as a metaphor for technology, I am indebted to Dr. T. David Gordon, author of *Why Johnny Can't Preach* (Phillipsburg, NJ: P & R Publishing, 2009), for telling me the following joke: "When I'm gardening and my wife asks me, 'What are you making?' I always answer, 'Blisters!'"
5. John Culkin, "A Schoolman's Guide to Marshall McLuhan," *Saturday Review*, March 18, 1967, 51.
6. Carr works through studies on the brain's "plasticity" in chapter 2 of *The Shallows: What the Internet Is Doing to Our Brains*, rev. ed. (New York: W. W. Norton, 2020), 17–35.
7. Marshall McLuhan, *Understanding Media: The Extensions of Man* (Cambridge, MA: MIT Press, 1994), 7.
8. "Life Expectancy by Age, 1850–2004," Information Please Database, Pearson Education, Inc., 2007, http://www.infoplease.com/ipa /A0005140.html (accessed April 10, 2011).
9. By the year 2000, the world infant mortality rate was cut down to a third of what it was in 1950. It dropped from 153 deaths per 1,000 births to 52. In the United States, there were only 6 deaths per 1,000 births in the year 2000. In contrast, prior to 1900 infant mortality

rates could be as high as 1 in every 3 births. United Nations, Department of Economic and Social Affairs, Population Division, *World Population Prospects: The 2008 Revision*, New York, 2009 (advanced Excel tables), http://data.un.org/Data.aspx?d=PopDiv&f=variableID:77.

10. David H. Hopper, *Technology, Theology, and the Idea of Progress* (Louisville: Westminster John Knox Press, 1991), 10.

Chapter 3: Reflection

1. Makoto Fujimura, *Art and Faith: A Theology of Making* (New Haven, CT: Yale University Press), 7.

2. Andy Crouch, *Culture Making: Recovering Our Creative Calling* (Downers Grove, IL: InterVarsity Press, 2008), 23.

3. Ken Myers, quoted in Stanley James Grenz and John R. Franke, *Foundationalism: Shaping Theology in a Postmodern Context* (Louisville: Westminster John Knox Press, 2000), 141–46.

4. Emil Brunner, *Christianity and Civilization* (London: Nisbet, 1948), 62.

5. A. Caliskan, J. J. Bryson, and A. Narayanan, "Semantics Derived Automatically from Language Corpora Contain Human-Like Biases, *Science* 356 (2017): 183–86.

6. If you're interested in further discussion, this field of study is called "Speech Act Theory" and was pioneered by John Austin in the 1960s.

7. Mary McCleary, "The Work of Our Hands," in *It Was Good: Making Art to the Glory of God* (Baltimore: Square Halo Books, 2007), 127.

Chapter 4: Definition

1. Saint Augustine, *Augustine in His Own Words*, ed. William Harmless (Washington, DC: Catholic University of America Press, 2010), 317.

2. Stephen J. Kline, "What Is Technology?" in *Philosophy of Technology: The Technological Condition: An Anthology*, ed. Robert C. Scharff and Val Dusek (Malden, MA: Blackwell, 2003), 210–12.

3. Neil Postman, *Technopoly: The Surrender of Culture to Technology* (New York: Alfred A. Knopf, 1992), 13.

4. At this point, I must express my deep indebtedness to Stephen

V. Monsma's more nuanced definition of technology as "a distinct human cultural activity in which human beings exercise freedom and responsibility in response to God by forming and transforming the natural creation, with the aid of tools and procedures, for practical ends and purposes." See Stephen V. Monsma, Clifford Christians, Eugene R. Dykema, et al., *Responsible Technology: A Christian Perspective*, ed. Stephen V. Monsma (Grand Rapids: Eerdmans, 1986), 19. Thanks to Tim Challies for working with me on shortening my definition. It only took twenty emails or so.

Chapter 5: Rebellion

1. Hebrew בָּרָא (*bara*): Gen. 1:1, 21, 27; 2:3, 4; 5:1, 2; 6:7.

2. Hebrew יָצַר (*yatsar*) Gen. 2:7, 8, 19.

3. Hebrew עָשָׂה (*asah*): Gen. 1:7, 11, 12, 16, 26, 26, 31; 2:2, 3, 4, 18; 3:1, 7, 14, 21.

4. Other translators argue that the text should read "garments *for* their skin" rather than "garments *of* skin." In either case, God is still creating.

5. Jacques Ellul, *The Meaning of the City*, trans. Dennis Pardee (Grand Rapids: Eerdmans, 1993), 11.

6. From the Latin *homo incurvatus in se*. Saint Augustine, *Lectures on Romans*, trans. Wilhelm Pauck (Louisville: Westminster John Knox Press, 2006), 112, 159. http://mis.kp.ac.rw/admin/admin_panel/kp_lms/files /digital/SelectiveBooks/Theology/Luther%20-%20Lectures%20 on%20Romans%20(Library%20of%20Christian%20Classics).pdf.

7. Saint Augustine, *The City of God*, trans. Marcus Dods, 14.13, accessed from https://ccel.org/ccel/schaff/npnf102/npnf102.iv.XIV.13.html.

8. Blaise Pascal, *Pensées*, trans. W. F. Trotter, II:139, https://ccel.org/ccel /pascal/pensees/pensees.iii.html.

9. Again, we are not attempting to make the biblical story about the origin of tools and or map this story to any archaeological accounts. We are simply affirming that the Bible is truthful and allowing others to sort out the details.

10. Steve Jobs, in his speech accepting the Golden Plate Award from the Academy of Achievement in Washington, DC, 1982.

Chapter 6: Approach

1. Marshall McLuhan, *Understanding Media: The Extensions of Man* (Cambridge, MA: MIT Press, 1994), 17–18.

2. Langdon Winner, *The Whale and the Reactor: A Search for Limits in an Age of High Technology* (Chicago: University of Chicago Press, 1988), 103.

3. D. M. Studdert et al., "Handgun Ownership and Suicide in California," *New England Journal of Medicine* 382, no. 23 (June 2020): 2220–29.

4. Leo Marx, "Technology: The Emergence of a Hazardous Concept," *E-Technology and Culture: The International Quarterly of the Society for the History of Technology* 51, no. 2 (July 2010), http://etc.technologyand culture.net/2010/08/technology-a-hazardous-concept/.

5. Zachary A. Geller, "Are You With Me? The Impact of Losing a Conversation Partner's Attention to a Mobile Device," *CUNY Academic Works*, accessed March 12, 2022, https://academicworks.cuny.edu /gc_etds/2321.

6. Neil Postman, "Five Things We Need to Know About Technological Change" (lecture, Denver, CO, March 28, 1998), https://web.cs .ucdavis.edu/~rogaway/classes/188/materials/postman.pdf.

7. Marshall McLuhan and Eric McLuhan, *Laws of Media: The New Science* (Toronto: University of Toronto Press, 1992).

8. See Chris Martin, *Terms of Service: The Real Cost of Social Media* (Nashville: B&H, 2022).

Chapter 7: Redemption

1. Exodus 20:3–5. Jews, Roman Catholics, and some Lutherans enumerate the Ten Commandments differently, putting these two commandments together. In either case, the following points are the same.

2. Neil Postman, *Amusing Ourselves to Death: Public Discourse in the Age of Show Business* (New York: Penguin, 1985), 9. Emphasis in the original.

3. See, for example, Kate Ott's *Christian Ethics for a Digital Society* (Lanham, MD: Rowman & Littlefield, 2018), and Shannon Valor's *Technology and the Virtues: A Philosophical Guide to a Future Worth Wanting* (New York: Oxford University Press, 2018).

Chapter 8: Mediums

1. Phone usage patterns and social conventions change over time, as seen in Claude S. Fischer's book *America Calling: A Social History of the Telephone to 1940* (Berkeley: University of California Press, 1994).

2. Ivan Illich, *Tools for Conviviality* (London: Marion Boyars, 2021), 28.

3. Marc Prensky, "Digital Natives, Digital Immigrants," *On the Horizon* 9, no. 5 (October 2001), http://www.marcprensky.com/writing/Prensky%20-%20Digital%20Natives,%20Digital%20Immigrants%20-%20Part1.pdf.

4. Heidi Campbell, *Digital Creatives and the Rethinking of Religious Authority* (New York: Routledge, 2021).

5. Tish Warren Harrison, *Liturgy of the Ordinary: Sacred Practices in Everyday Life* (Downers Grove, IL: InterVarsity Press, 2019), 29.

6. For a more detailed analysis of changes in biblical interpretation, see Marshall McLuhan and Eric McLuhan, *Laws of Media: The New Science* (Toronto: University of Toronto Press, 1992), 218. Thanks to Joseph Kim for letting me see an early version of his dissertation, "Marshall McLuhan's Theological Anthropology," Dallas Theological Seminary, 2010.

7. The Hebrew Old Testament had various numbering and organizing systems for quite some time before chapter and verse numbers were added to the Greek New Testament.

8. Peter M. Phillips, *The Bible, Social Media and Digital Culture* (New York: Routledge, 2020).

9. Shane Hipps, *Flickering Pixels: How Technology Shapes Your Faith* (Grand Rapids: Zondervan, 2009), 76.

10. The original source of this idea has been difficult to trace, but it did appear online in this article: Justin E. H. Smith, "On the Internet,"

Berfrois (blog), January 7, 2011, http://www.berfrois.com/2011/01
/on-the-Internet/.

11. For scientific quantification of how pornography uniquely interacts
with the human brain, see William M. Struthers, *Wired for Intimacy:
How Pornography Hijacks the Male Brain* (Downers Grove, IL: InterVarsity Press, 2009).

12. Tim Challies, *The Next Story: Life and Faith after the Digital Explosion*
(Grand Rapids: Zondervan, 2011), 199.

13. Sharon Begley, "I Can't Think!" *Newsweek*, February 27, 2011, http://
www.newsweek.com/2011/02/27/i-can-t-think.html.

14. Eric Schmidt, interview by Charlie Rose, *Charlie Rose*, June 9, 2016,
https://charlierose.com/videos/28222.

15. Victor M. González and Gloria Mark, "Constant, Constant, Multi-
tasking Craziness: Managing Multiple Working Spheres," Proceed-
ings of ACM CHI '04: Conference on Human Factors in Computing
Systems (Vienna, Austria, April 26–29, 2004), 113–20.

16. Cardinal Robert Sarah, *The Power of Silence: Against the Dictatorship of
Noise* (San Francisco: Ignatius Press, 2017), 56.

17. Matthew Lee Anderson, "Three Cautions Among the Cheers: The
Dangers of Uncritically Embracing New Media" in *The New Media
Frontier: Blogging, Vlogging, and Podcasting for Christ*, ed. John Mark
Reynolds and Roger Overton (Wheaton: Crossway, 2008), 63.

18. Girl Scout Research Institute, *"Who's That Girl?* Image and Social
Media Survey" and *"Who's That Girl* factsheet" (New York: Girl Scouts
of the USA, 2010), http://www.girlscouts.org/research/publications
/stem/image_and_social_media_survey.asp.

19. Sherry Turkle, *Alone Together: Why We Expect More from Technology and
Less from Each Other* (New York: Basic Books, 2011). Turkle has written many books on the positive aspects of social networks, but she
says *Alone Together* was a kind of "repentance" for leaving out the more
negative influences it can have. Also see Ira Flatow, "Have We Grown
Too Fond of Technology?" NPR, February 25, 2011, http://www.npr
.org/2011/02/25/134059283/have-we-grown-too-fond-of-technology.

20. Leisa Reichelt, "Ambient Intimacy," March 1, 2007, *disambiguity* (blog), http://www.disambiguity.com/ambient-intimacy/.

21. Sigmund Freud, *Civilization and Its Discontents* (New York: W. W. Norton, 1961), 38.

22. Mark Sayers, *Facing Leviathan: Leadership, Influence, and Creating in a Cultural Storm* (Chicago: Moody, 2014), 127.

23. It's important to distinguish between the "icon" used in early Christian worship and the "images" we use today. Icons are deliberately unrealistic so that they can direct the viewer away from the icon itself and point toward a spiritual reality. In contrast, images are designed to be as realistic as possible. Eastern Orthodox worship permits icons but not images, while Catholic worship requires images. Thanks to Dr. T. David Gordon for this distinction. The point I am making here is that the early church thought deeply about the theological meaning of the mediums they employed in worship.

24. St. John Damascene, *On Holy Images*, trans. Mary H. Allies (London: Thomas Baker, 1898); available at http://www.fordham.edu/halsall /basis/johndamascus-images.html.

Chapter 9: Restoration

1. Saint Augustine, *Quaestiones in Heptateuchum* VII. 2.73: PL 34, 623.

2. Some scholars have argued that, in reference to Joseph and Jesus, the word *tektōn* should be translated "stonemason" rather than "carpenter" because Jesus grew up in Nazareth at the time when the nearby city of Sepporus was being built. The main material in the region was stone instead of wood, and Sepporus was built from that stone, so its builders would have employed masons instead of carpenters. Of course, there is no way to know for certain whether the kind of *tektōn* ("skilled work") that Joseph did was that of carpentry or masonry, but in either case, Jesus's death involved woodwork, and his resurrection involved stonework.

3. Jacques Ellul, *The Meaning of the City*, trans. Dennis Pardee (Grand Rapids: Eerdmans, 1993), 173.

4. N. T. Wright, *Simply Good News: Why the Gospel Is News and What Makes It Good* (New York: HarperOne, 2017), 96.

5. Some passages in which the idea of "in person" or "face-to-face" is mentioned are Acts 25:16; Rom. 1:11; 1 Cor. 13:12; 2 Cor. 10:1; Gal. 1:22; Col. 2:1; 1 Thess. 2:17; 3:10; 2 Tim. 1:4; 4:9; 2 John 12; 3 John 13–14.

6. Chris Cox, quoted in Geoffrey A. Fowler, "Facebook's 'Social' Chief Pushes Human Interaction," *Wall Street Journal* online, October 10, 2010, http://online.wsj.com/article/SB10001424052748704127904575544302659920236.html.

7. Neil Postman, "Five Things We Need to Know About Technological Change" (lecture, Denver, CO, March 28, 1998), https://web.cs.ucdavis.edu/~rogaway/classes/188/materials/postman.pdf.

Chapter 10: Technicism

1. David Noble, *The Religion of Technology: The Divinity of Man and the Spirit of Invention* (New York: Knopf, 1997), 4.

2. Kevin Kelly, *What Technology Wants* (New York: Viking, 2010), 148.

3. The One Laptop Per Child (OLPC) project was created by Nicholas Negroponte to bring low-cost, networked laptops to children in impoverished countries with the hope that access to information and development of computer skills would contribute to solving problems in those countries.

4. Saint Augustine, *The City of God*, trans. Marcus Dods (New York: Modern Library, 2000), 14.28, 447.

5. Stephen V. Monsma et al., *Responsible Technology*, ed. Stephen V. Monsma (Grand Rapids: Eerdmans, 1986), 50.

6. Francis Bacon, *The New Organon* (Indianapolis: Bobbs-Merrill, 1960), 39; quoted in Monsma, *Responsible Technology*, 84.

7. Friedrich Nietzche, *The Gay Science: With a Prelude in Rhymes and an Appendix of Songs*, trans. Walter Kaufmann (New York: Vintage, 1984), 181.

8. This is not meant to argue against theistic evolution, only to argue

against a purposeless form of evolution driven by accidental chance rather than divine intention.

9. Ray Kurzweil, "The Evolution of Mind in the Twenty-First Century," in *Are We Spiritual Machines? Ray Kurzweil vs. the Critics of Strong A.I.* (Seattle: Discovery Institute, 2002), 53.

10. Michael DeLashmutt attempted to ask this very question to several people in the information technology industry, but they did not openly use such terms to describe technology. DeLashmutt, "A Better Life Through Information Technology? The Posthuman Person in Contemporary Speculative Science," *Zygon* 41, no. 2 (2006): 267–88.

11. Anders Sandberg, "Why We Should Fear the Paperclipper," February 14, 2011, http://www.aleph.se/andart/archives/2011/02/why_we _should_fear_the_paperclipper.html.

12. For more Christian reflection on Artificial Intelligence, see Jason Thacker, *Age of AI: Artificial Intelligence and the Future of Humanity* (Grand Rapids: Zondervan, 2020).

13. Joshua Smith, *Robot Persons: Our Future with Social Robots* (WestBow Press, 2021).

14. For more Christian reflection on transhumanism, see Jacob Shatzer, *Transhumanism and the Image of God* (Downers Grove, IL: InterVarsity Press, 2019).

15. For a much more nuanced discussion of the connection between democracy, classical liberalism, and technology, see Murray Jardine, *The Making and Unmaking of Technological Society: How Christianity Can Save Modernity from Itself* (Grand Rapids: Brazos, 2004).

16. Please don't misunderstand this as criticism of Apple or Apple products. I quite enjoy them, and in fact I wrote myself a reminder on my iPhone to add this note. I am only pointing out that the creators of the Apple logo were very explicit in portraying technology overcoming human fallenness. For a more detailed analysis of Apple's logo, see Andy Crouch, "A World Without Jobs," January 19, 2011, https:// andy-crouch.com/articles/a_world_without_jobs.

17. The story of John Romulus Brinkley is told in the documentary film *Nuts* (2016).

18. Joseph Turow, *The Voice Catchers: How Marketers Listen In to Exploit Your Feelings, Your Privacy, and Your Wallet* (New Haven, CT: Yale University Press, 2021).

19. "Productivity" is calculated by comparing the value of the goods workers produce to the value of the goods they consume during production. An infographic on the subject can be found at http://www.good.is/post/does-technology-make-us-more-productive-workers/.

20. Ruth Schwart Cowen, *More Work for Mother: The Ironies of Household Technology from the Open Hearth to the Microwave* (New York: Basic Books, 1985).

Chapter 11: Virtualization

1. Albert Borgmann, *Technology and the Character of Contemporary Life: A Philosophical Inquiry* (Chicago: University of Chicago Press, 1984), 40–47.

Recommendations

1. David H. Hopper, *Technology, Theology, and the Idea of Progress* (Louisville: Westminster John Knox Press, 1991), 113.

2. Eric Brende, *Better Off: Flipping the Switch on Technology* (New York: HarperCollins, 2005), 134.

3. *Daily Mail*, "The Tiny Cage That Will Save Their Lives: Capsule Built to Hoist Trapped Chilean Miners Up Through 2,330ft of Rock Arrives," last updated September 27, 2010, http://www.dailymail.co.uk/news/article-1315342/Trapped-Chilean-miners-cage-built-hoist-2-330ft-rock.html.

INDEX

development in, 43, 64, 98, 137, 171–72
Eve, 56, 77, 114; clothing of, 78–81, 110

Facebook, 46, 106, 162, 187, 192
faithfulness, 144, 185, 206, 212; of God, 117–18
Farish, William, 70
Freud, Sigmund, 147

garden of Eden, 51–52, 55–56, 84–85, 158
God, 20–22, 149–50; and the creation of Jerusalem, 157–59; and the creation of the universe, 47–50; curses of, 80–81, 84; faithfulness of, 117–8; and the "first" technology, 78–79; laws of, 117–19; redemptive program of, 110–14; and the use of images, 122–23; and the use of technology, 31, 33, 44, 82, 89, 164–67
Grenz, Stanley, 53, 55, 67

Hipps, Shane, 139–40
Holy Spirit, the, 82, 117, 150, 193
Hopper, David, 45, 212
humanity, 42, 44, 50, 59, 174, 177

images, 53, 101, 118–19, 139–41, 229n23; importance of, 122–23; of Jesus, 149–50
information, consumption of, 41

Jerusalem, 156–59
Jesus Christ, 32, 44, 86, 113, 144, 149–50, 159–60, 229n2; return

of, 152–53, 173; as technologist and transformer, 153–55
Jobs, Steve, 89, 99, 166
John, 33–34, 83, 106, 158–60
John of Damascus, 150
Joseph (New Testament), 62, 153, 229n2
Joseph of Arimathea, 155
Joshua, 121

Kay, Alan, 24, 221n1
Kline, Stephen J., 67, 95
Kurzweil, Ray, 174

language, 53, 56–59, 114–16; importance of the Greek language, 155–56; programming, 46
Law of Moses, 117, 119
Lopez, Oscar, 127–28
Ludd, Ned, 178,
Luddites, 177–78
Luther, Martin, 27, 138

Marx, Karl, 95–96
Marx, Leo, 96
McLuhan, Marshall, 41–42, 93; on the four things all technology does, 103–4
media ecology, 100–3
mediums, 222n9; and the communication of meaning, 131; and the creation of culture, 134–36; definition of, 129; and difficulty, 132–33; and formality, 131–32; and speed, 133; and representation, 133–34
mediums, and the shaping of thinking and behavior, 137; digitally, 144–49; through photography, 139–42; through the internet,

141–44; through the printing press, 137–39
metaverse, 191, 195, 197
Monsma, Stephen, 73, 171, 225n4 (ch. 4)
Moses, 117–18, 119

Nietzsche, Friedrich, 173–74
Noah, 110–13
non-fungible tokens, 195
Nye, David, 37

Old Testament, organization of, 227n7
online churches, 105–6

Pascal, Blaise, 87
Paul, 34, 106, 156, 161
Peter, 160, 161, 199
Plato, 63, 222n12
pornography, 141, 228n11
Postman, Neil, 29, 69–70, 100, 123, 162
productivity, and prosperity, 183–85

rebellion, 77, 79, 86, 159, 160, 165, 218
redemption, and technology, 33, 82, 110, 113, 118, 125, 158, 217, 218–19
reflection, 49, 50, 52, 55, 59, 62, 78, 79, 81–82, 97, 115, 164–66, 218; and embracing our role, 59–60
Reichelt, Leisa, 147
restoration, 33, 48, 110, 118, 151–52, 161–62, 165–67, 177, 217, 219; of Jerusalem, 157; of Peter, 160, 199; spiritual, 82, 150, 155–58

Schmidt, Eric, 143
sin, 50, 78–79, 81, 82, 85, 86, 87, 107, 112, 113,

ABOUT THE AUTHOR

JOHN DYER (PhD, Durham University) has been a web developer for more than twenty years, building tools used by Apple, Microsoft, Harley-Davidson, and the Department of Defense. He currently serves as the VP of Enrollment and Educational Technology and Assistant Professor of Theological Studies for Dallas Theological Seminary and lives near Dallas, Texas, with his wife, Amber, and two children, Benjamin and Rebecca. He has written on technology and faith for Gizmodo, *Christianity Today*, and The Gospel Coalition, and in several other books. You can find out more about his coding and writing at https://j.hn/.